Manu, Gandhi and Ambedkar
and Other Essays

MANU GANDHI and AMBEDKAR
and Other Essays

MADHU LIMAYE

GYAN

GYAN PUBLISHING HOUSE

NEW DELHI-110002

Manu, Gandhi and Ambedkar

ISBN : 9788121204873

Reprint in 2016 in India by
Gyan Publishing House
5 , Main Ansari Road, Daryaganj,
New Delhi - 110002
Phone : 9811692060

E-mail : books@gyanbooks.com
gyanbook@vsnl.com
Website: gyanbooks.com

CONTENTS

Preface

SECTION I

CASTE AND SOCIAL JUSTICE

1. Campaign to Malign Gandhi Must Stop 3
2. Gandhi versus Ambedkar : A Futile Controversy 11
3. Ambedkarism: Fake and Genuine 16
4. Who is More Relevant : Gandhi-Ambedkar or Kanshiram and his Ilk? 21
5. Manu, Gandhi and Ambedkar 25

SECTION II

THE GATT DEBATE

6. Globalisation and the West's Non-Economic Weapons 35
7. The Gatt Final Act and Communist Orthodoxy 41
8. A Policy for India in a Cruel World 47
9. Socialists : Selling Stale Bread 52
10. Marxists : Worship of Obsolete Dogmas 57
11. Anti-Gatt Front: A Non-Starter 62
12. Work Ethos and Development 66
13. Must Competition Breed Concentration? 72

SECTION III

CONSTITUTIONAL AND PARLIAMENTARY CONTROVERSIES

14. Who killed the Unanimous JPC Report? 81
15. Legislatures' Oversensitiveness on the Question of their Privileges 93
16. A Welter of Judicial Decisions 98
17. Will Expanded State Autonomy Help? 105
18. Sheshan's War on Carpet-baggers 109
19. Endless Elections Cause Administrative Paralysis 114
20. Multi-member Bodies, Election Commission and the Constitution 118
21. Electoral Reform Bills : An Analysis 122
22. Restructuring the Election Commission: A Plea for Common Sense 126

SECTION IV

POLITICS OF 1994

23. The BJP at the Forking of Roads 133
24. Is the Congress in Irreversible Decline? 138
25. Denizen of the World of Make Believe 146
26. Why do the Regional Parties Endure? 152
27. The BJP's New Ploy 165

SECTION V

INDO-RUSSIAN RELATIONS

28. American Fear of a German-Russian Entente 171
29. Narasimha Rao's Russian Visit: An Assessment 175
Index 179

PREFACE

This is a collection of my writings in the first half of the current year. The subject matters of these essays are the burning issues that have agitated public opinion from the beginning of the new year. (There is only one essay written in 1993).

The first part deals with the issue of social justice in a caste society. The first essay was written after Kanshiram and Ms. Mayavati of the Bahujan Samaj Party resumed their false and malicious propaganda campaign against Mahatma Gandhi. It is not surprising that men like V.P. Singh, whose only stock-in-trade is the vote bank politics kept quiet. What has caused me deep pain is that the so-called Gandhians, Sarvodayis and my Socialist colleagues have also observed deafening silence on this issue.

Another question that "rocked" the press and Parliament—if not the broad masses—was the Gatt Final Act. The debate, on both sides, barring a few exceptions, was ill-informed. Most parliamentarians and party activists have neither read the Final Act nor do they understand the changing contours of the global economy nor the deep impact of the knowledge and information revolution that is sweeping through the world. I have set out my own position in the second part of this book.

The third part of this volume takes up the controversies touched off by the decisions of the constitutional authorities like the Supreme Court, the positive actions—and also antics—of the Chief Election Commissioner, the policies of the Central Cabinet, Parliament's consideration of important Bills relating to electoral reforms, the functioning of the Election Commission and the Legislatures as also their oversensitiveness in the matter of their privileges. Then there is my detailed commentary on the unique report of a Special Joint Parliamentary Committee on the Stock Market Scam.

The fourth part deals with the fortunes of political parties, including regional parties, and the contradictions and conflicts that assail them. These pieces provide the background to the series of Assembly elections which would take place towards the year's end or the beginning of the next.

The last part takes a fresh look at Indo-Russian relations in the context of the collapse of the Soviet System in 1991.

The book has used the original versions of the essays and not the shortened versions published in the press.

I thank my friends Dr. Haridev Sharma, Narayan Shetye and my wife, Champa Limaye, for the help they have given in preparing the press copy and reading the proofs.

31 July 1994 **Madhu Limaye**

Section I

CASTE AND SOCIAL JUSTICE

1

CAMPAIGN TO MALIGN GANDHI MUST STOP

I have no hesitation in declaring that in the fight that is daily growing more intense between the forces of social justice and equality on the one side and the partisans of the age-old privilege rooted in a hierarchical order based on birth, I am wholly and unreservedly on the side of the OBCs, SCs and STs. But I view with apprehension the tendency of certain leaders of the oppressed to defame Mahatma Gandhi day in and day out for no rhyme or reason. I am myself an admirer of Mahatma Phule, Narayan Guru, Periar, Dr. Ambedkar, Dr. Lohia and other champions of a casteless society. But my admiration for these leaders does not require me to abuse Gandhi who was "a universal leader of suffering humanity". He championed the cause of the Scheduled Castes, Scheduled Tribes, women, poor kisans and exploited labourers. He stood for peace and harmony among the different religious communities of India. He gave the oppressed and unarmed people the powerful weapon of civil disobedience. Like Dr. Ambedkar he was a strong advocate of universal suffrage, and wanted the Scheduled Castes, Scheduled Tribes and women to be given the right to vote. To falsely allege, as some leaders of the Scheduled Castes and OBCs have done, that "Gandhi had opposed in 1931-32 the Shudras being given right to vote and that when they were given the vote by the British, on 18 August 1932, Gandhi undertook a fast." It is just not true that the British Government granted universal franchise to the Scheduled Castes, Scheduled Tribes and the OBCs. They did not. Churchill had told Ambedker that adult franchise was not a practical proposition. In fact the British people themselves had achieved adult suffrage after a determined struggle which lasted more than a century and half.

Perhaps, the leader who made these blatantly untruthful charges, had based himself on hearsay and was not aware of the true position. If that is so, he should quickly correct himself. But if he has made the charge knowing full well that it was not true, I can only say that such "malice afore thought" will not help the oppressed people to whose liberation from the shackles of Brahmanical social order he says he is dedicated.

Let me now juxtapose the attitude of Dr. Ambedkar and Mahatma Gandhi on the franchise issue. When the Montford Reforms were on the anvil Dr. Ambedkar passionately argued before the Southborough Committee on Franchise in favour of a low-pitched franchise for the Scheduled Castes. Taking into account "the grave position of the untouchables", Dr. Ambedkar said that they must aim at lowering the franchise. It was wrong to confine the franchise only to those who could "be expected to make an intelligent use" of it, for "the exercise of vote was itself an education".[1]

Nearly a decade later Dr. Ambedkar appeared before the Simon Commission and he linked his acceptance of joint electorate with adult franchise. The following exchange is instructive:

Colonel Lane Fox:

> In each memorandum you ask for special representation for the depressed classes. You ask for adult suffrange... It is obvious it is a bigger thing if you ask for it for the aborigines and criminal tribes and so on. Are these privileges asked for the bigger figure or for the smaller?

Dr. Ambedkar:

> I ask for them for the depressed classes.

Colonel Lane Fox:

> For the aborigines and criminal classes also?

Dr. Ambedkar:

> No. I do not think it would be possible to allow them the privilege of adult suffrage... We claim reserved seats if accompanied by adult franchise.

Chairman:

> And if there is no adult franchise?

Dr. Ambedkar:

> Then we would ask for separate electorates.[2]

As late as May 1945 Dr. Ambedkar continued to oppose adult suffrage and reserved seats for the Aboriginals on the ground that "these Aboriginal Tribes do not yet possess the political capacity which is necessary to exercise political power for one's own good."[3] Dr. Ambedkar said that he did not claim to be a leader of all suffering people. Life was short and his own strength slender and so he had concentrated on the cause of Untouchables, although he acknowledged that there were other noble causes also.[4]

It would be interesting to examine the "solution" of the communal problem which Dr. B.R. Ambedkar had offered in 1945.

Dr. Ambedkar strongly denounced the appeasement of Muslim communalism by the British. He also deplored the liberal attitude of the Congress towards the Muslims, which was influenced chiefly by its desire to present a united front. There were no limits to Muslim demands and there were no limits to concessions, Ambedkar said. He wrote:

> A demand is made for separate representation on a population basis. That is conceded. Next, a claim is made for weightage in representation. That is granted. It is followed by a demand for statutory majority over other minorities with the right for the majority to retain separate electorates. This is granted. This is followed by a demand that the majority rule of another community is intolerable, and therefore

> without prejudice to its rights to maintain majority rule over other minorities, the majority of the offending community should be reduced to equality. Nothing can be more absurd than this policy of eternal appeasement. It is a policy of limitless demand followed by endless appeasement... On the other hand, there is a community economically poor, socially degraded, educationally backward and which is exploited, oppressed and tyrannized without shame and without remorse, disowned by society, unowned by Government and which has no security for protection and no guarantee for justice, fair play and equal opportunity.[5]

Then Ambedkar went on to outline his scheme of representation of various sections in the different Legislatures. By way of illustration only the composition of the Central Assembly and a few other States, with a significant adivasi (Scheduled Tribes) population, under the Ambedkar Scheme, is given below:

Central Assembly[6]

Community		*Percentage of Representation*
Hindus	...	40
Muslims	...	32
Scheduled Castes	...	20
Indian Christians	...	3
Sikhs	...	4
Anglo-Indian	...	1
Bihar		
Hindus	...	40
Muslims	...	30
Scheduled Castes	...	28
Indian Christians	...	2

Community		*Percentage of Representation*
	Assam	
Hindus	...	40
Muslims	...	39
Scheduled Castes	...	19
Indian Christians	...	2
	Orissa[6]	
Hindus	...	40
Scheduled Castes	...	36
Muslims	...	22
Indian Christians	...	2

About the shocking total non-representation of the adivasis under his scheme, Ambedkar wrote:

> It will be obvious that my proposals do not cover the Aboriginal Tribes although they are larger in number than the Sikhs, Anglo-indians, Indian Christians and Parsees. I may state the reasons why I have omitted them from my scheme. The Aboriginal Tribes have not as yet developed any political sense to make the best use of their political opportunities and they may easily become mere instruments in the hands either of a majority or a minority and thereby disturb the balance without doing any good to themselves.[7]

Ambedkar's whole idea was to enhance the representation of the Scheduled Castes at the expense of the Savarna Hindu (traivarnikas as well as *Shudras*) and the adivasis. He clearly wanted to put the Scheduled Castes in a position, where they could play the balancing game between the Caste Hindus and Muslims, through manipulation of weightages and representation. It was a blatantly sectional approach and extremely unjust to the adivasis or Scheduled Tribes or aboriginals as he called them. Thakkar Bapa of Gokhale's Servants of India Society and a close associate of Gandhi in his anti-Untouchability Campaign and adivasi welfare strongly protested against Ambedkar's ignoring the Scheduled

Tribes through letters to *The Times of India*. Ambedkar's contention that the Scheduled Tribes (adivasis) were uneducated did not wash. He himself had argued before the Southborough Committee that the exercise of the right to vote was itself an education. Besides, although Ambedkar did not know this, there were among the S.T.s. many educated and qualified men like Jaipal Singh of South Bihar. Dr. Ambedkar's slighting of adivasis was an index of the narrowness of spirit which, of course, had its origin in the millenia-old *Savarna* oppression of the so-called *panchamas*. The free India's Constitution, however, rightly put the adivasis on the same footing as the Scheduled Castes in the matter of vote, of representation in the Legislatures, reservation in educational institutions and in the services. Mahatma Gandhi called himself a saviour of the Scheduled Castes or Harijans, but he was a friend of the poor and the lowly in general—Harijans, the Scheduled Tribes, Criminal Tribes, and Backward Classes, handicraftsmen, weavers and all the rest of them. He was a benefactor of the human race, a universal saviour. To malign such a man, and call him a *Manuvadi* and enemy of Dalits is not only preposterous but despicable. It is a sure sign of a twisted mind.

Mahatma Gandhi was opposed to separate electorates for the Scheduled Castes, but he was definitely for giving all of them the right to vote. The Resolution on Fundamental Rights and Economic Changes passed at the Karachi Congress in 1931 was mainly drafted by Gandhiji and among the fundamental rights enumerated therein were *the rights to adult suffrage, free primary education and freedom from serfdom.*[8] At the Calcutta Session of the Congress in 1928 Gandhi supported the Nehru Report which had demanded adult suffrage. In an article in *Young India*, 16 July 1931, Gandhi endorsed the Congress scheme on the communal problem which had laid down that the *franchise shall be extended to all adult men and women, and that joint electorate shall form the basis of representation in the future Constitution of India.*[9]

Gandhi told the Federal Structure Committee of the Round Table Conference that he was "wedded to adult suffrage.... Adult suffrage is necessary for reasons more than one; and one of the decisive reasons to me is that it enables me to satisfy all the reasonable aspirations, not only of the Musalmans, but also of the so-called untouchables, of Christians, of labourers and all classes." Gandhi said that he could not restrict vote to wealth or literacy, "for some of the finest specimens of humanity were to be found amongst the poorer people and amongst the untouchables themselves." If the knowledge of the three R's were made a condition of franchise, "I shall have to wait until the Greek Kalends, and I am not prepared to wait all that time."[10]

In his discussion with Harold Laski, J.F. Horabin, H.N. Brailsford and others Gandhi said on 3 December 1931 that *he would not be satisfied without adult suffrage. At a stroke I arm the untouchables with tremendous power.*[11]

Not all Mahatma Gandhi's ideas were fixed from the beginning of his life to its end. Except the principle of non-violence and the ideal of the service of suffering humanity, on other matters Gandhi was not only open to change, but as matter of fact he did evolve and change in the course of his long public career. The defender of the Varna system in his early days reversed himself so completely that he became an enthusiastic supporter of the Savarna-Harijan and inter-community marriages without conversion. It behoves us therefore to acknowledge the services of and draw strength from all those—Thakkar Bapa is one of them—who helped the oppressed. From the day the Constitution came into force Thakkar mounted a relentless pressure for the implementation of the provisions relating to the OBCs, SCs, STs. We should, therefore, gratefully remember those who fought for the oppressed and depressed classes in their own way, and not revile them.

It was Gandhi's influence that led many leaders to accept adult suffrage and give reserved seats to the SCs and STs in proportion to their population (Article 330 of the Constitution of India). More than one-fifth of the Lok Sabha members come from these groups. *We can no more hold Gandhi's defence of Varna system in his early stages against him than we can hold Dr. Ambedkar's opposition to adult franchise and representation for the Adivasis and the so-called Criminal Tribes in the period from 1928 to 1945 against him*. The Constitution which Dr. Ambedkar piloted gave equal treatment to the Scheduled Castes and Scheduled Tribes both in the matter of reserved seats in the Lower Houses of the Legislatures as well as reservation in the services. The nation must therefore honour both the Mahatma and the Doctor.

References

1. *Dr. Babasaheb Ambedkar's Writings and Speeches*, Vol. 1, pp. 255 and 267.
2. *Ibid*, Vol. 2, pp. 463-65.
3. *Ibid*, Vol. 1, pp. 357-79.
4. *Source Material on Dr. Ambedkar*, Vol. 1, pp. 297-98 and 300-301.
5. *Dr. Ambedkar's Writings and Speeches*, Vol. 1, p. 366.
6. *Ibid*, pp. 369 and 371.
7. *Ibid*, p. 375.
8. *Collected works of Mahatma Gandhi*, Vol. 45, p. 371.
9. *Ibid*, Vol. 47, pp. 139-141.
10. *Ibid*, Vol. 48, pp. 31-32.
11. *Ibid*, p. 384.

2

GANDHI VERSUS AMBEDKAR: A FUTILE CONTROVERSY

I confess that I am much distressed by the controversy that has been raised by the BSP leaders on the historical role of Mahatma Gandhi in the struggle for social justice. I particularly regret the highly violent and offensive language which is being used by the BSP spokesmen. They are denouncing him as enemy of the Scheduled Castes and Backward Classes. This is a travesty of truth. Rank prejudice cannot be equated with conclusions based on a deep study and research. They presume to speak in the name of Dr. B.R. Ambedkar. But they forget that Dr. Ambedkar put knowledge and learning above everything else. He was also an enemy of hero worship. He thought that "hero-worship was demoralising for the devotee and dangerous to the country." I early realised the inequity of the caste system, and became an admirer of Dr. Ambedkar ever since my college days despite the fact that the general press was then hostile to him.

There was undoubtedly a sharp difference of outlook between Mahatma Gandhi and Dr. Ambedkar. But an objective evaluation of their roles cannot but lead to the conclusion that both were working towards the same goal, of course, in their own different ways.

It would not be out of place to recall certain facts. Before the advent of Mahatma Gandhi the Congress as such had never concerned itself with social problems. However in the early days of the Indian National Congress there used to assemble, alongside of the Congress Session, a sitting of the Social Conference, and no conflict had arisen between the two till the followers of Tilak opposed the holding of the Social Conference in the Congress pandal in 1895. That was the end of the Social Conference as an adjunct of the Congress. Within two decades the position was wholly reversed : in 1919-20 Gandhi transformed the Congress itself into an instrument of *both* political and social change. Gandhi intensified his fight for social reform in 1932-33.

Gandhi had asked Ambedkar (in 1933) to send him a message for publication in the first issue of his new Journal, *Harijan*. Ambedkar said:

> The outcaste is a bye-product of the caste system. There will be outcastes as long as there are castes. Nothing can emancipate the outcaste except the destruction of the caste system. Nothing can help to save Hindus and ensure their survival in the coming struggle except the purging of the Hindu faith of this odious and vicious dogma.[1]

Dr. Ambedkar contended that caste was a notion; it was a state of mind. The destruction of the caste must therefore mean a notional change, a mental revolution. The real remedy must begin with the destruction of popular belief in the Shastras. People must be won over to an egalitarian outlook.

Gandhi disputed Ambedkar's statement that untouchability would not go without destruction of *Varnavyavastha*. Personally he would restrict himself to the fight against untouchability. It was highly likely that at the end of it they should find that there was nothing to fight against in Varnashram. If, however, Varnashram even then looked an ugly thing, the whole of Hindu society would fight it. *Humility and an open mind were Gandhi's lovable qualities. He closed his reply to Ambedkar with these words : "At the end of the Chapter, I hope that we shall all find ourselves in the same camp".*[2]

There was another debate between Gandhi and Ambedkar on the question of temple entry in the same year. Gandhi appealed to him to make an unbiased study of Hinduism and if it failed "to sustain him in the hour of need, by all means let him forsake it." On his own part, Gandhi thought that Harijans deeply felt the denial to them of the right of temple-entry. It was for thousands of them a serious deprivation : "The betterment of their economic and educational conditions is undoubtedly required. But no betterment of those conditions will give religious equality. That cannot be attained even by statute, but only when the heart of the caste Hindus is changed."[3]

Making an allusion to India's past and its inability to preserve its freedom, Dr. Ambedkar said that "only when the Hindu society becomes a casteless society that it can hope to have strength enough to defend itself...." He made a fervent appeal to the Hindus to reflect on whether they should conserve the whole of their heritage or select what was helpful and transmit to future generations only that much and no more. Ambedkar was however emphatic that the only remedy for breaking caste was intermarriage. "Nothing else will serve as solvent of caste.... Fusion of blood alone can create the feeling of being kith and kin. Without this feeling of being kindred caste cannot vanish".[4]

Notwithstanding his initial fascination for *Sanatana Dharma* Gandhi could not long ignore the real weakness of Hindu society. Long years ago he had declared war on the evil of untouchability. It was the exigencies of this war which forced Gandhi to expand the front of his battle against the petrified structure of Hindu Society. The ceaseless struggle against untouchability drove him to oppose all attempts to detach the depressed classes from the Hindu fold. He staked his life to fight separate electorates, but once his main objective was secured, he showed readiness to negotiate a generous settlement with the Scheduled Castes on the question of representation. It was again the logic of his determination to root out untouchability, to which he sincerely and ardently subscribed from the very inception, that drove him to attack the other citadels of Hindu exclusiveness, and particularly taboos about marriages and eating without giving up either his vegetarianism or his sound tenets about personal cleanliness or hygiene. Gandhi thus came to wrestle finally with the inherent contradiction in his position. He had to abandon his belief that Hindus should only ply their ancestral occupation or marry within caste. When he finally discarded *Varnashram* based on birth, he not surprisingly began to approve inter-caste, *Savarna-Harijan* marriages as well as inter-communal marriages. His own son married a Brahmin and Gandhi gave his blessing to the union.

It needs to be emphasised that Gandhi before his death by assassination had come to the same position as Ambedkar had taken at the beginning of this great debate. I must also point out that in the pre-independence days Dr. Ambedkar was not only opposed to giving the adivasis adult franchise but even representation in the Legislatures. Just as Gandhi discarded his old views on the Varna system, so later Dr. Ambedkar too modified his stand on the issue of the Scheduled Tribes.

Let me now turn to the framing of the Constitution. It is well-known that the Congress had effective control over the Constituent Assembly. But it did not place its party interest above the nation's interest. It inducted into the Constituent Assembly eminent non-Congressmen. Dr. Ambedkar himself was brought into it by Sardar Patel. The pivotal role of the Congress in Constitution-making was stressed by Dr. Ambedkar himself. Dr. Ambedkar confessed that his election as Chairman of the Drafting Committee pleasantly surprised him. He pointed out that it was the disciplined functioning of the Congress which made the smooth passage of the Draft Constitution possible.

The Constitution has placed into the hands of the oppressed masses powerful weapons like universal suffrage, reserved seats in the Legislatures for the SCs and STs, Articles 15 and 16 relating to educational opportunities and reservation in employment under the state and other weapons. All this became possible because Gandhi taught the Congress to place social justice at the centre of its policy. Gandhi was not an enemy of Dalits, minorities, OBCs and women as the BSP leaders allege. He was their greatest benefactor.

The advocates of social justice have ignored the developing conflicts *between* the OBCs on the one hand and SCs on the other as also the contradictions within the OBCs, SCs and STs over economic interests and power-sharing. *Unless these are resolved and a comprehensive platform created there is a danger of internal disruption and the SP-BSP electoral performance in UP turning into a Pyrrhic victory. Mere slogans and violence of language will not do.*

References

1. *CWMG*, Vol. 53, pp. 259-60; the first issue of *the Harijan weekly* was published on 11 February 1933.
2. *Ibid*, pp. 259-61.
3. *Ibid*, p. 307.
4. Dr. B.R. Ambedkar, *The Annihilation of Caste*, Third Edition, p. 54.

3

AMBEDKARISM : FAKE AND GENUINE

There always has existed in India a tribe of Gandhi baiters. Particularly was it noticeable in Western India in the pre-freedom days. The members of this tribe with Hindu Mahasabhaite, Savarkarite and RSS background were a particularly odious lot. The Brahmanical pride of some of them was deeply hurt by the emergence of Gandhi. They thought it scandalous that a mere Bania should presume to give them lessons in politics. *Nathuram Godse was only the most violent, pathological and repulsive specimen of this tribe.*

BJP's former Chief Minister of Uttar Pradesh Kalyan Singh probably considers himself a greater, wiser and more perceptive person than Netaji Subhas Chandra Bose. It was Netaji who reverentially addressed Gandhi as Father of Our Nation. But now Kalyan Singh hotly disputes the honorific which Netaji conferred on Gandhiji, and refuses to acknowledge him as the creater of the modern Indian nation.

The most astonishing and painful thing is the vicious tirade the BSP's Kanshi Ram and his lieutenant Mayavati have launched against Gandhi. Elated by their success in winning a little over five dozen seats in the large UP Assembly—and that, too, in alliance with Mulayam Singh's Samajavadi Dal, the twosome have thrown all sense of proportion to the four winds. Their ceaseless cataract of invective can bring no benefit to the Scheduled Castes. It might, in fact, bring great harm on them. It is a pity that all this is being done in the name of Dr. B.R. Ambedkar.

Ambedkar was a highly literate leader and a great votary of

knowledge. He accorded education the highest priority. But these neo-Ambedkarites exult in their ignorance and prejudice. The false prophets and spurious champions of social justice amongst us have deliberately ignored this campaign for they fear that their defence of Gandhi would erode their vote banks. Their new mantle of prophethood conceals the inner core of power politics and power hunger. But truth must prevail.

It is quite true that when the British influence was paramount in India many sections of the population looked to them for aid and comfort. The Muslim League did that, so did the communal-minded Christians and Sikhs. Some Non-Brahmin groups also leaned on British power. Only the small Parsi community refused to invoke their aid. As to the Depressed Classes, their condition was the most miserable and it was not a matter of surprise that they should appeal to the British rulers to safeguard their interests under the new constitutional dispensation. Dr. Ambedkar fully shared in the polemics and party warfare of that period and did everything in his power to protect the Depressed Classes. But when the British finally decided to transfer power and quit, a big change came and Dr. Ambedkar was pragmatic enough to realise the bankruptcy of the old politics of the Depressed Classes. He accepted the conciliatory offer of Sardar Patel and cooperated in the framing of Constitution. All the safeguards that he wanted, such as reservation of seats in Legislature, adult franchise as a pre-condition of joint electorate, reservation in education and services and abolition of Untouchability and its practice being treated as an offence, were provided by the new Constitution which he helped to frame.

The relevant thing today is not Ambedkar's pre-freedom anti-Congress and anti-Gandhi polemics, but his objective appraisal of Gandhi's role after 1948. In his last 18 months Gandhi waded through rivers of hate and violence, and sought to bind the nation's festering wounds. He himself fell a victim to this campaign of hate.

Ambedkar was aware of Mahatma Gandhi's multiple services in India's cause. Most Indians respected him as the leader of the national liberation movement. A large number revered him as a saintly figure. A few Westerners thought of him as the most

Christ-like figure that had ever walked on earth. Some looked upon Gandhi as the new prophet of non-violence. But even before the achievement of freedom Ambedkar thought it self-evident that Gandhi valued far more "his reputation as the savior of Untouchables than his reputation as the champion of Swaraj or as the protagonist of Ahimsa."[1]

Ambedkar was pessimistic about the disappearance of Untouchability. The reason for this pessimism was his analysis of this unparalleled evil phenomenon. Speaking on the Third Report of the SC-ST Commissioner in the Rajya Sabha on 6 September 1954 Dr. Ambedkar said :

> What is untouchability ? Let us understand it very carefully. Untouchability, so far as I understand it, is a kind of a mental disease of Hindus... it is a mental twist; every Hindu believes that to observe untouchability is the right thing... I cannot see how you blame the Hindus. For thousands of years, by the teaching of this dirty law they have got inculcated in their mind the doctrine that untouchability is a most sacred thing... He must not touch this, he must not touch that, he must not eat this, he must not eat that, etc.... That is the position and all that we can do is to see that untouchability which, as I said, is a mental twist of the Hindus does not protrude so much into public life as to involve the civil liberties of the people.[2]

Dr. Ambedkar therefore thought that the evil itself would take years and years to vanish, for it was a question of "mental twist". But "there was no reason why we should not strongly agitate for seeing, whether untouchability goes or not, that the social, economic, political and constitutional rights of the Scheduled Castes are fully protected."[3]

Then Ambedkar made a startling suggestion which needs to be set out fully. He suggested revival of the Salt tax which had been abolished in memory of Mahatma Gandhi. When abolished the revenue was Rs. 10 crores and if restored, now (1954) it would be Rs. 20 crores. *"I respect Gandhi," he said and requested the Government to revive it and "create a Gandhi Trust Fund for the welfare of the Scheduled Castes, for their development and settlement."* Ambedkar *said "after all the untouchables, according to all of us, were the nearest and dearest to him," and he would certainly bless from heaven the scheme created for the "people whom he wanted to protect and to elevate."*[4]

Gandhi revolted against pollution and untouchability when he was only 12 year old, and held it to be a sin. His own humiliating experience in South Africa fully opened his eyes to the plight of the Untouchables, who had, for millennia, daily and hourly, suffered degradation. Gandhi's personality was completely different from that of Ambedkar. Gandhi consciously cultivated calmness and inner poise. As Lajpatrai said he was a master of polite expression. He put his case with great skill but with studied moderation. Ambedkar on the other hand argued his case with unusual vigour and force. He did not mind having recourse to exaggeration. Hyperbole was for him quite in order.

A South African critic of Gandhi, who later became Gandhi's most intimate colleague in South Africa, wrote on 26 December 1896 that the bulk of the Indians labouring class in South Africa belonged to the low castes who were condemned to servility by the caste system. "It was an evil within. Whosoever wished to improve the condition of his fellowmen must first address himself to the removal of the evil within." The barbed arrow "penetrated to the core" of Gandhi's heart: "The truth burst upon his mind with the force of revelation that so long as India allowed a section of her people to be treated as *pariahs,* so long must her sons be prepared to be treated as *pariahs* abroad. To destroy the twin evil of "untouchability" and insanitation root and branch became his passion. So seared was his soul that as a token of expiation for the treatment meted out to the "outcastes" he ultimately took to scavenging, declaring that India's independence could wait but not the eradication of the curse of "untouchability".[5]

Being a deeply religious person Gandhi did not use the expression mental twist but called it a sin embedded in the inner core of a Hindu. The two expressions signified the same thing. He knew eradication of this evil was not alone a matter of some constitutional or socio-economic measures. It involved a transformation of the warped Hindu mind. The analysis and the solution of both Gandhi and Ambedkar was similar. The appraisal of both of them differed from the opinion of Gandhi's close intellectual colleague, Jawaharlal Nehru, with his pre-occupation with the concept of "the foundation of economic relations and superstructure based on it". That close colleague had as late as 1952 grandly declared : "I do not recognize that there is such a problem as that of the untouchables. There is a general problem of the economically poor and the problem of the untouchables is a part of that problem. It will take its place and receive its attention along with the other problems. There is no occasion, no purpose in bestowing any special thought upon it".[6]

Neither Gandhi nor Ambedkar could swallow this preposterous proposition which was also advanced by other Marxist intellectuals and leaders. Most of us Socialists, guided by Rammanohar Lohia, joined the camp of Mahatma Phule, Mahatma Gandhi and Dr. Ambedkar. I therefore say : Fellowmen and women from the SCs, STs and OBCs, beware of the fake Ambedkarites. Embrace the real Ambedkar, a conscience keeper of Gandhi.

References

1. *Dr. Babasaheb Ambedkar's Writings and Speeches*, Vol. 9, pp. iv-v.
2. *Rajya Sabha Debates*, 6 September 1954; *Dr. B.R. Ambedkar's Speech on the Report of the Commissioner of Scheduled Castes and Scheduled Tribes for 1953*, Columns. 1664-65.
3. *Ibid*, Col. 1474.
4. *Ibid*, Col. 1472.
5. *Mahatma Gandhi The Early Phase*, Vol. I, Pyarelal, Ahmedabad, 1965, pp.476-478.
6. *Rajya Sabha Debates, 6 September 1954*, Column 1473.

4

WHO IS MORE RELEVANT: GANDHI-AMBEDKAR OR KANSHIRAM AND HIS ILK?

It is a matter of deep regret that the various organizations of the Scheduled Castes or Depressed Classes or Harijans—or whatever expression you please—are unable to unite on the basis of an agreed programme of social justice as part of the larger platform of national regeneration and integration. Most of the political outfits have regional following; none has succeeded in becoming a truly national organization. Prakash Ambedkar, grandson of B.R. Ambedkar, has his Bahujan Maha Sangh, but it is largely confined to Vidarbha, Nagpur, Marathwada and some other parts of Maharashtra. There are in Maharashtra other rival Republican groups also. Rambilas Paswan has his Dalit Sena and he has some following in Bihar, UP and other places. The Bahujan Samaj Party (BSP) of Kanshiram, Mayavati and their lieutenants is the largest of the Dalit organizations. But their victory in five to six dozen constituencies in Uttar Pradesh (the total Assembly strength is 425) has absolutely turned their heads and they are assuming that they are about to sweep into political power in all parts of India and at the Centre. Even assuming that all the Scheduled Castes support the BSP—which of course is quite untrue—their total vote would not be more than 17 per cent. How can they capture political power at the Centre on the basis of this slender support?

In fact by preaching day in and day out hatred and daily humiliating friends and allies, the BSP is unwittingly laying the basis for a fratricidal war. Only a blind person or an ignoramus is unaware of contradictions between the OBCs and Scheduled Castes, between the Scheduled Castes and Scheduled Tribes and internal conflicts and rivalries between these three groups themselves. So far nobody, yes, nobody, has undertaken a serious campaign to resolve these conflicts of interest—economic conflicts, contention over power sharing and distribution of reservation benefits, as also quarrels over social ranking and status. Ambedkar perceptively spoke of an ascending scale of respect and reverence and a descending scale of contempt under the caste system based on birth. With the exception, perhaps, of Mulayam Singh nobody is even bothered about these conflicts.

Championship of sectional causes and singing hymns of hate extract a fearful price. I am sorry, I cannot call this promotion of enmity among the non-*traivarnikas* new political consciousness or constructive awakening.

Innumerable instances can be given of these internecine conflicts and bloody clashes. The Jats and Jatavas (Chamars) are in perpetual tension in areas from Bharatpur to Agra. In Saharanpur the Gujars—an OBC group—murdered a Harijan boy—or a Scheduled Caste boy if you please—and a Gujar girl, for making a love marriage. There is going to be no conviction of those arrested because nobody would come forward to give evidence for fear of retaliation by the caste panchayats.

In another place in UP, the Sainis—a caste not very unlike the Kushwahas and Malis—both OBCs—of a village bumped off a Yadava boy and a Saini girl because they committed the unpardonable sin of falling in love and getting married. Again the persons arrested will go scot free after a trial which would be for all practical purposes farcical.

In South Bihar a Harijan youth was killed and a Kurmi girl stripped and humilated because they had eloped and married.

There are numberless instances of clashes between Yadavas and Dalits, between Kurmis and Dalits. There is rivalry between Yadavas on the one hand and Kurmis and Koiris (Kushwahas) on the other.

The most painful report of these internecine conflicts has come from Orissa. I think it necessary to give a fair summary of this.

It should open the eyes of the admirers of the so-called "new awakening", if not of the deliberate and conscious flatterers and sycophants :

> **Phulbani, May 13**
>
> Orissa's coldest district has been burning with tribal fury for the past few months with the outnumbered Harijans being at the receiving end. Clashes between the two communities in several villages have left at least four Harijans dead and scores of others injured.
>
> The rows of empty houses and the panic-stricken faces in Harijan *bastis* belie the official claim that all is back to normal. "We can't sleep anymore. The tribals are still holding secret meetings and chalking out plans to attack us" said Somanath Behera of Balaskumpa village. The residents fear an attack as soon as the police picket is withdrawn.
>
> Nearly 500 Harijan families had fled their homes to escape tribal attacks last fortnight and taken refuge in Phulbani town. Several have been returned, but many more families are arriving from the remote areas where there is no police protection. ...
>
> Underlying the enmity between the two communities is a feeling among tribals, reinforced by politically motivated propaganda by a section of the ruling Janata Dal, that the Harijans have managed to corner all the benefits because they enjoy political power.[1]

Mahatma Gandhi was not a sectional leader. He was a universal benefactor, especially of the poor and lowly. His was a message of love, of mutual adjustment and conflict resolution. B.R. Ambedkar, though he called himself only a champion of the Scheduled Castes, was a worshipper of knowledge. *He knew the ultimate key to power is knowledge. We have entered a knowledge society. Hymns of hate will not bring any results*. But who cares? We have some academics who declare that both Gandhi and Ambedkar are no more relevant! It is only leaders like Kanshiram and Mayavati, who wallow in ignorance and hate, who are really relevant in our age. *As to the academics, who run institutions with a liberal dose of the oxygen of foreign funding, and who somehow manage to win favour with all the parties in power, they are even more relevant than the BSP leaders, not to speak of Gandhi and Ambedkar!* For who does not know that one such academic wangled a hefty sum from an External Affairs Minister and held a World Disarmament Conference which in terms of results did not produce even a mouse after digging a mountain. This academic also ingratiated himself to the Janata Dal leadership and got into the Planning Commission. The Industry Minister of this Government, Ajit Singh, laid an Industrial Policy Statement in Parliament, obviously not as a personal statement, but as a document approved by the Prime Minister and the Cabinet. This academic member of the Planning Commission declared a war on this Industrial Policy statement, without showing the decency of resigning his membership from the Planning Commission which is not an elected body, but an appointive one.

Worshippers of the Rising Sun often come to a bad end. Not many years ago the newspapers were full of Tikait and stories of the rising farm power. Nobody hears much of Tikait these days. Kanshiram won a victory of sorts in UP, but that was in alliance with Mulayam Singh's Samajvadi Dal. Of course the Samajvadi Dal also profited by the tie-up. But the arrogance which this little victory has generated is absolutely confounding. In the current UP bye-elections, however, Kanshiram and Mayavati are not much visible. Why? It is about time the well wishers of the Dalits, adivasis, minorities and OBCs restrained the new Messiahs from running down Gandhi. Mahatma Gandhi's place in history is assured. His traducers very likely will not even get a footnote in history.

References

1. *The Times of India*, 14 May 1994.

5

MANU, GANDHI AND AMBEDKAR

It is a matter of great surprise to me that some academics and writers with Marxist leanings, have come out in defence of the BSP's leaders' false propaganda against Gandhi. For long years the North India's Scheduled Castes were strong supporters of the Congress, because they thought that leaders like Babu Jagjivan Ram and the Congress Party to which he belonged were the inheritors of the Mahatma's legacy. It was only in some Western UP pockets that Jatavas were Ambedkarites and backed leaders like B.P. Maurya. In the 1979-80 Lok Sabha elections the Janata Party had projected Babuji as the future Prime Minister. I remember that Jatavas (or Chamars as they are known in Eastern UP and Bihar) had for the first time broken away from the Congress and had voted for a non-Congress Party—the Janata Party. Mrs. Gandhi was able to retain her Harijan base in the 1977 election throughout the country, because the "Amma" had established close rapport with them. She retained that sympathy in the South even in 1977-80. In the Chikmaglur bye-election, despite the lavish amounts the Janata Party spent on the campaign, it made not the slightest impact on the OBCs, SCs, and the minorities. Jagjivan Ram's meetings were thinly attended and audience had to be procured for him. The mass instinct is never wrong in judging what leader really loves them and what leader only exploits them because of their vote potential. I don't think the Scheduled Castes much loved either Jawaharlal or Rajiv Gandhi for they knew that neither had any understanding of their inhuman condition nor had any real desire for their uplift. For both of them they were just a part of the poor mass. I once happened to watch on TV Rajiv Gandhi receiving a delegation of Scheduled Castes from Haryana at a friend's home.

(I have no TV set and don't watch it). He asked their leaders to hand over their memorandum to some official. His attitude was one of total indifference. He did not even look at the large group which had come to see him with great hope. His mother would have behaved completely differently in a situation like this. She would not have bothered about time, would have walked up to them, and talked to men and, especially, women and even lifted up a child or two. Of course Mrs. Gandhi was not unfamiliar with the technique of histrionics. But it was not all a hypocritical show. She did have, I can tell from personal experience, a genuine sympathy for the Depressed Classes and the tribals and harboured distrust of powerful farming communities like the Jats, the Patidars and the Marathas.

What love could the Scheduled Castes people, who often saw Rajiv Gandhi on TV, have for Jawaharlal's grandson? Jawaharlal himself never had any sympathy for Gandhiji's anti-untouchability campaign. He wrote in his *Autobiography* : "But social reform, the Sarda (Child Marriage Restraint) Act and the Harijan Movement did not fill our—means his—mind, except in so far as I felt a little irritated by the Harijan Movement because it had come in the way of civil disobedience." He naively thought that it was "not very difficult to convert the masses to social reform if the state takes the matter in hand."[1] The state did take these matters in hand, but what has been the result? I have seen babies in arms being married off in Rajiv's own Amethi constituency during the Lok Sabha bye-election he fought after Sanjay Gandhi's death. Nor has the condition of the rural Depressed Classes, the tribals, Annexure I OBCs, village women, and especially, Muslim women much improved.

Ambedkar called Untouchability and Caste a mental twist of the Hindus; and Gandhi called it a sin of which the non-removal would spell the ruin of Hinduism. The two used different language, but their meaning was the same. Both were in favour of economic, political and educational measures, but what they, above all, wanted was the untwisting of the mental knot and purging of the sinfulness and genuine repentance.

I doubt whether Kanshiram and Mayavati have either read

Manu or Ambedkar or Gandhi. Even if they had not read Manusmriti, because of lack of grounding in Sanskrit, they can consult G. Buhler's famous translation. Manu forbids Pratiloma marriage and although he makes allowance for a high caste person taking lower caste women as additional wives, the first wife has to be from his own caste. Not only that, the progency of the other varna (or caste) wives is given a low status. They are not treated as Brahmanas or Kshatriyas.[2] I do not wish to dilate on the disgraceful treatment prescribed by Manu for the "lower Castes" and his shameless glorification of Brahmins except to say that Manu wanted Shudra's name to express something contemptible and denote service or *dasyabhava*.[3]

Emerson once declared that "consistency is the virtue of an ass." Gandhi valued truth and humanity more than verbal consistency. He changed his views and discarded the old ones if he considered them to be wrong. So did Ambedkar whenever he thought the old attitudes and opinions would hinder the cause of the welfare of the Depressed Classes to which he was devoted. Ambedkar always thought inter-marriages on a mass scale was the only solvent of Caste.

I shall cite only two statements of Gandhi, less than eighteen months before his death, which would show that he sought to uproot the foundations of the Law of Manu.

A Correspondent from a Shimla Hills State informed Gandhiji in September 1946 that a young man from a high caste Hindu family married a Koli (OBC) girl. The Raja Saheb sentenced the couple to six months' imprisonment and a fine of Rs. 100 each. The Correspondent thought this repressive act was intolerable and retarded progress.

Gandhiji after quoting the aforesaid letter said that one-man rule was intolerable and must go. He hoped that the couple which this Correspondent had mentioned, would "cheerfully undergo the sentence. Only many should follow their example, if the tie is not lustful bondage, but a bond of love born out of the zeal for reform. If the reformers do not wish to suffer imprisonment, they should migrate to a free place where they can live without let or hindrance."[4] Can a Manuvadi write like that?

A Patidar friend suggested to Narhari Parikh, Gandhi's associate, that if an educated Harijan girl married a Caste Hindu boy the couple should devote itself to the service of the Harijans. Gandhi's opinion was sought on this. Gandhi expressed his agreement and said that not self-indulgence but love and service should be object of such marriage. Then he went on to expound his radical view on the subject in these words :

> Even if one Harijan girl marries a caste Hindu with a high character it will do good to both the Harijans and caste Hindus. They will set up a good precedent and if the Harijan girl is really worthy, she will spread her fragrance far and wide and encourage others to copy her example. Society will cease to be scared by such marriages. They will see for themselves that there is nothing wrong in them. If Children born of such a union turn out to be good, they will further help to remove untouchability. Every reform moves at the proverbial snail's pace. To be dissatisfied with this slowness of progress betrays ignorance of the way in which reform works.
>
> It is certainly desirable that caste Hindu girls should select Harijan husbands. I hesitate to say that it is better. That would imply that women are inferior to men. I know that such inferiority complex is there today. For this reason I would agree that at present the marriage of a caste Hindu girl to a Harijan is better than that of a Harijan girl to a caste Hindu. *If I had my way I would persuade all caste Hindu girls coming under my influence to select Harijan husbands.* That it is most difficult I know from experience. Old prejudices are difficult to shed. One cannot afford to laugh at such prejudices either. They have to be overcome with patience. And if a girl imagines that her duty ends by marrying a Harijan and falls a prey to the temptation of self-indulgence after marriage, the last state would be worse than the first. The final test of every marriage is how far it develops the spirit of service in the parties. *Every mixed marriage will tend in varying degrees to remove the stigma attached to such marriages. Finally there will be only one caste, known by the beautiful name Bhangi, that is to say, the reformer or remover of all dirt. Let us all pray that such a happy day will dawn soon.*[5]

Does a Manuvadi think like this? Manu would most certainly have tortured Gandhi for writing this and would have sent him to hell forever!

The hatred of Kanshiram and Mayavati for Gandhi is as deep as their ignorance of the writings of Manu, Ambedkar and Gandhi is colossal.

If Manu had written his Code in terms of the above passage of Gandhi or Ambedkar's famous manifesto on *Annihilation of Caste* India would have become the greatest country in the world. It was against the background of these revolutionary views of Mahatma Gandhi that Sardar Patel wrote on 15 April 1948 to Dr. Ambedkar when he married a Brahmin Doctor, Savita Kabir, that if Bapu had been alive today he would have given you his blessings on your marriage. Ambedkar heartily concurred. "I agree that Bapu, if he had been alive, would have blessed" the marriage.[6] Not only this. When Ambedkar saw Pyarelal walking near the present Khadi Bhandar on the Outer Cannaught Place road, some days later, he got down from his car and expressed his sorrow that Bapu was not alive to give his blessings. Regretfully he said: "We did not understand him." It was Ambedkar's greatness that he saw the nobility of Gandhi's soul and buried the old hatchet.[7]

In 1954 Ambedkar paid Gandhi the highest complement by saying that "all of us"—that is including Ambedkar himself—knew that the Dalits were the nearest and dearest to him.[8]

But I know that it is futile to argue with these BSP men. They are saying and doing everything with carefully weighed deliberateness. Their aim is to disrupt the forces of national unity, industrial and agricultural development and economic equality.

But it is not the BSP which is alone to blame for Gandhi-baiting and neglecting the broader aspects of the social problem. The Communists were also at one time Gandhi-baiters. They and Nehru talked only of the class problem and economics. Others are now falling into the opposite error. *Some non-BSP parties are harping on reservation as the panacea for all our ills.* After four years' noise and din, only one OBC officer has been recruited in the Central

Government Services. Meanwhile, the internal conflicts within the camp of those who stand by social justice are tearing apart the broadbased front which had been painfully put together in North India as a result of the efforts initiated by Dr. Rammanohar Lohia decades ago.

Some utterances of Kanshi Ram fill me with dismay. *Thus Kanshi Ram has loudly proclaimed that he is against reservation.* His Party would be in a position to grant reservation to others. He made it clear that he was not craving for Muslim support either.[9]

At the Lucknow rally on 10 July 1994 he attacked the Dalit IAS and IPS and said that they were exploiting the SCs.[10] Earlier at Kanpur, the BSP's supreme leader, addressing a Kushwah rally, had said that in UP there were 550 IAS officers out of which the Dalits were 112. But the number of OBCs was only seven. He blamed Gandhi for this state of affairs.[11] But could the Dalits have attained this position without the Constitution framed by Gandhi's men? Could this progress have been made without the help of Articles 15, 16, 46, 330, 332, 335,338 and so on.?

All this talk of Kanshi Ram must be dismissed as cheap bravado. For it is quite clear that the abolition of reservation would constitute a terrible setback to the Depressed Classes, although it is quite true that reservation is *only one among the many remedies* that needed to be applied for the solution of the problem of social inequality. Kanshi Ram of late has been attacking not only Gandhi but also Ambedkar. He says that he is greater than Ambedkar. Gandhi had reduced Ambedkar to a leader of Mahars (a Scheduled Caste of Maharashtra).[12] But this was not true of him. Kanshi Ram's greatness, he asserted, lay in the fact that he had the Dalits with him and had crushed Gandhi's progeny to pulp. This kind of approach and the brinkmanship he recently practised in UP, I am afraid, are not likely to abolish Caste and Manuvad. It would only aggravate the internecine conflict.

The unfortunate part is that not one or two but several OBC and kisan castes and STs and SCs are involved in these conflicts. If the new OBC, SC and ST consciousness means intensified fatricidal war, then the fate of the ideal of an egalitarian society is wellnigh sealed.

Similarly, unless social justice is married to land reforms and a revolution in agricultural production and its diversification, and also a rapid increase in the output of energy and all other sectors of industry, not only will the aforesaid conflicts get intensified but the growing criminalisation of public life will dissolve our hard won ordered state into an 18th century type anarchy and chaos.

References

1. *Jawaharlal Nehru, An Autobiography,* New Delhi, 1980, p. 384.
2. *Bulher, The Laws of Manu,* III, pp. 14-18.
3. *Ibid,* II, pp. 31-32.
4. *Harijan,* 6 September 1946, (*CWMG,* Vol. 85, p. 402).
5. *Harijan,* 7 July 1946, *CWMG,* Vol. 84, pp. 388-89.
6. *Sardar Patel's Correspondence,* (Ed. Durga Das), Vol. 11, p. 327.
7. Pyarelal to Dr. Haridev Sharma of the NMML.
8. *Rajya Sabha Debates,* 6 September 1954, column 1472.
9. *The Telegraph,* 12 July 1994.
10. *The Times of India, 11 July 1994.*
11. *Jansatta, 6 April 1994.*
12. *The Telegraph, 12 July 1994.*

Section II

THE GATT DEBATE

6

GLOBALISATION AND THE WEST'S NON-ECONOMIC WEAPONS

Sometime during the twelfth century the countries to the West of Vistula *awakened* to their existence not only as a group of Christian peoples but as members of a distinctive Western Christian Commonwealth held together by the Catholic Church with its head in Rome. They invented the Gothic Cathedral—Saint Dennis near Paris was the first architectural structure—the symbol of their soaring curiosity and ambition. The Western Christian Commonwealth, which had now outgrown its barbarism, was a dynamic society. An unprecedented burst of energy took the Westerners to the four corners of the earth. In its explosive impact on the course of human history, the Western dominance surpassed the Arab expansion in the centuries following the unification of the Arab tribes under Islam.

Inventiveness and aggressiveness were the hallmarks of this new force. The Western people's *Crusades* devastated large parts of the domains of two civilisations : Orthodox Christian civilization, with its capital in Constantinoples and the Levant under Muslim Turkish rule. The Crusades failed, but only after embittering relations between the Western Christians and followers of the Greek Orthodox Church as also relations between Christians and Muslims. The part of the Iberian Peninsula under Muslim rule was forcibly rechristianised.

By now the Western countries had travelled far on the road to technological progress. In ship building and navigation they rapidly forged ahead enabling them to undertake voyages of discovery,expand commerce and colonise vast spaces in the Americas.

With the invention of firearms and improvements in artillery and military organization, the West was able to achieve superiority in land warfare also. The failure of the seige of Vienna by the Ottoman Turks in 1529 was symbolic of the irreversible decline of the Islamic civilization and the beginning of the worldwide ascendency of the West.

Since the establishment of its worldwide ascendency, the West has used every Economic and Non-economic theory, principle and device—the Cross, Mercantilism, Free Trade, Protectionism, Human Rights, Campaign Against Child Labour, Sanitation, Social Correctness and Environment to perpetuate its dominance, which rests, in the last analysis, on superior force. The Protuguese and the Spaniards, like the Crusaders, picked up the Cross and established their maritime empire in the name of Christ, the king of Peace.

The doctrine of free trade is associated with Britain. But Britain did not always support free trade. Earlier, it subscribed to the Merchantalist Theory and Practice and invoked state intervention to strengthen its position. The British textile industry was so alarmed by the import of Indian cotton fabrics that a Bill was introduced in the House of Commons (1696) to prohibit Indian textiles. Indian fabrics were such a rage that a contemporary ditty said:

> Our Ladies all were set a gadding,
> After these Toys they ran a madding...
> And like gay Peacocks proudly strut it,
> When in our streets alone they foot it.

It was only when Britain became the World's Workshop that it began to see great virtue in free trade. But Germany, the United States and Japan did not subscribe to Free Trade. They were protectionist and continued to be so for a long time. However, defenceless India, whose economy was entirely self-sufficient, was forcibly sucked into the vortex of new relations with Britain and could neither protect its old industries nor start new ones with state help.

The Free Trade doctrine suffered a setback in the inter-war period. After the Great Depression, most countries became protectionist. Nazi Germany's Autarchy and Stalin's Socialism in One Country were extreme attempts to insulate the national economies from the impact of the World Economic Crisis.

The Protectionist policies continued after the War. The Common Market (now European Union) is a Protectionist Combine. With the new revolution in materials and substitutes, and knowledge and information, Free Trade seems to be on the march again. But neither Americans, nor the European Union nor Japan really wish to open up their economies. They wish to use the Uruguay Final Act, to be signed on 15 April 1994, as a lever to force open the Third World countries which practise various forms of Protectionism : China's State Socialism, the mixed economy and high tariffs of India and other countries.

As for the powerful and advanced industrial countries, there is not the slightest chance that they will *honestly* follow free trade policies and give the developing countries access to their markets. For they have ready at hand other weapons, theories, principles and instruments to bludgeon the weak developing nations. The West can never be hauled up on the ground of "discriminating treatment in international trade relations." *For it will adopt not the traditional trade weapons, but the more effective extra-trade devices.*

There is the doctrine of human rights. Who can deny that it is a beautiful and noble cause? Invoke it and you can shut out the products of countries violating these rights. The Western countries, of course, never suppressed human rights. There never was slavery in the United States nor lynching nor discrimination against the blacks. The Western Civilization, we are to believe, never produced Nazism and Fascism or apartheid. It was just a bad dream.

Then there is the humanitarian movement against forced labour or child labour. What humanist or civil libertarian can object to anybody's harking to it? The mighty Chinese Republic had to accept the humiliating condition of allowing a team of Americans to inspect its five prisons which were supposed to manufacture products dumped on the American market!

The French and probably other EU countries would like to close their shores and borders to Indian-made carpets which employ child labour—surely a loathesome practice! Britain and France, naturally, never employed children in their factories. One may ask, what of the miserable condition of children described by Charles Dickens and H.G. Wells? But all these were novels and these, and even the Blue Books, on which Marx draws heavily, must be regarded as imaginative literature and not the reflection of the actual industrial conditions! Any way the West had achieved civilised standards long back and was it not its sacred duty make others conform to these standards? The most effective way to teach is to keep carpets produced by children out of the EU market.

Then there are of course the minimum standards of sanitation and hygiene. These can certainly be called in to help keep out the dirty and unhygienic products of the developing countries which do not observe the necessary health and hygiene regulations. The Final Act itself has provisions on sanitary and phyto-sanitary regulations and these would be used to beat the developing world. Are not the agriculturists of the developing countries using pesticides, certainly, produced by the West, but which it has now pronounced harmful? How can we admit into our markets these contaminated products? Two Annexes of the Final Act spell all this out. Can it be doubted that this is a sound reason, for thë entire medical science will endorse it.

Recently, the European countries have invented a new progressive doctrine in defence of "Social Correctness". The "principal tenet is that it is no longer acceptable to carry on liberal trade relations with any country failing to provide its workers with 'adequate social protection.' Such countries are said to be engaged in the practice of 'social dumping,' as their lower labour costs enable them to undercut countries in economic competition that do provide proper social protection.... In order to raise their competitors' production costs, the socially correct seek to impose their system of labour relations, workplace regulations, employment and remuneration laws, and social security provisions, all the while maintaining that they do so in the interest of universal workers' rights." How can our trade union internationalists oppose Social Correctness?

But this is not all. Preservation of the human habitant, ecology and environment is another Western concern, and therefore a potent weapon of the developed countries. What if their economics and defence programmes have in the past done the greatest harm to the human habitant? What if the Western States' reckless squandering of the earth's finite resources have inflicted the greatest damage on the biosphere? What if the US is responsible for the highest rate of emissions (20 tonnes per person)? Now the Western countries have awakened to the danger and would like to make available to the developing countries the fruits of their experience and wisdom. If the Third World does not listen, then, of course, sanctions would have to be forged to make the lesser breeds see reason and persuade them not to continue to produce goods in a manner as would add to pollution.

This is the World we live in. The collapse of the Soviet Union and the Warsaw Pact have created a situation where ignoring the noble principles, doctrines and theories of the World Leader is fraught with the greatest danger. I confess that both the ecstacy of those who rhapsodise globalisation and free market and the lamentations of those who mourn the loss of economic sovereignty leave me cold.

Those Dunkelites who are euphoric over liberalisation and globalisation will realise that nothing has changed as far as the Indian bureaucracy and the Army of Inspectors is concerned. The indigenous industry used to a sheltered market for over four decades will be rudely jolted and will end up as auxiliaries of the Transnationals. Some, seeing the writing on the wall, have already made settlements on "good terms". Others will follow suit. Efficient enterprises would, however, survive and profit by the stimulus of competition.

Private sector is not free from blemish. The owners neglected efficiency, and never tried to lower costs. They looted the consumers. They concentrated on lobbying and not on industrial innovation. They forgot that protection breeds complacency, inefficiency and cartels." For those who only lament, self-introspection is out of the question. They love to wallow in self-pity. Why do they ridicule our private sector pigmies? Did we not cripple them for thirty years by restricting their productive capacities? Did we not view with suspicion the growth in the assets and turnover of Big Business Companies? We discouraged work ethos and efficiency among workers. We encouraged overstaffing, absenteeism and malingering and looked down upon hard work. Was not increase in factory output like poison to the Marxist trade unionists? Was not enhanced profitability a sin? Was not the productivity-linked wage hikes a blasphemy? We throttled the private sector on ground of principle, and we allowed the greed and corruption of managers *and* employees to destroy the public sector and nationalised credit institutions. *We hoped that the public sector would succeed despite the total lack of public spirit and enterprise and excess of red tape and bureaucratism.* I am afraid our people are sold on Consumerism. When non-economic factors like status, fashion, pressure to conform, social approval or disapproval and so on become operative, for the affluent section anyway price is no consideration at all. Even those who cannot afford the price, will purchase these goods at the cost of essentials. In brief, while the supporters of Dunkel are naive and gullible, many of the opponents are hypocrites.

7

THE GATT FINAL ACT AND COMMUNIST ORTHODOXY

The Ministerial Declaration on the role of the new Multilateral Trade Organization (MTO) contained in the Final Act not unexpectedly poured libations to globalisation and liberalisation. But the libations were not generous. The reason is that the commitment of the United States, European Union and Japan to these goals is not genuine. A prestigeous economic journal observed: "Between the end of previous trade round (in 1979) and the beginning of the Uruguay round (in 1986), the industrial countries moved briskly towards greater protection.... The worry is that from now on the task of securing freer trade may grow more difficult, not less."[1]

And yet it was a famous mid-nineteenth century manifesto which had described the definitive triumph of Free Trade and World Market in almost ecstatic terms: "The bourgeoisie cannot exist without constantly revolutionising the instruments of production, and thereby the relations of production and with them the whole relations of society.... The need of a constantly expanding market for its products chases the bourgeoisie over the whole surface of the globe. It must nestle everywhere, settle everywhere, establish connexions everywhere. The bourgeoisie has through its exploitation of the world-market given a cosmopolitan character to production and consumption in every country. To the great chagrin of Reactionists, it has drawn from under the feet of industry *the national ground* on which it stood. All old-established national industries have been destroyed or are daily being destroyed. They are dislodged by new industries, whose introduction becomes a life and death question for all civilised nations, by industries that no longer work up indigenous raw material, but raw material drawn from the remotest zones; industries whose products are consumed, not only at home, but in every quarter of the globe. In place of the old wants, satisfied by the productions of the country, we find new wants, requiring for their satisfaction the products of distant lands and climes. In place of the old local and national seclusion and self-sufficiency, we have intercourse in every direction, universal interdependence of nations.... It compels all nations, on pain of extinction, to adopt the bourgeois mode of production...."[2]

Who sang this paean to the God Apollo in his incarnation as the Free Market Economy and the Globalisation of Production and Exchange? Was it some ideologist of the United States or of the World Bank or the International Monetary Fund? No, this hymn was sung by no less a person than Karl Marx. When the young Marx composed this song of Capitalism, the industrial revolution and the creation of an international market were really in an incipient stage. What Marx enthusiastically described in 1848 was more in the nature of the dominant tendency of the age and not its total realisation. His praise, then, must have sounded as an exaggerated rhetoric than an accurate description of the actual reality.

Throughout the second part of the nineteenth century and early part of the twentieth century, the process of industrial revolution and the creation of a world market continued to gather momentum. Apart from Britain and France, the US, Germany and, to an extent, Russia and Japan were also launched on the road to industrialisation. By 1914, it seemed that Marx's prediction about the establishment of a Global Economy was about to be dramatically fulfilled. However, the first World War and the subsequent revolutionary upheavals arrested abruptly the march towards the creation of a truly World Economy and globalisation of production and exchange. The economic difficulties and the unsettled conditions in the post-war world, followed by the Great Depression of 1929-32 forced the industrialised nations to adopt protectionism.

The pre-war tendency towards liberalisation and lowering of trade barriers received a set back. The Nazi Policy of autarchy (self-sufficiency) and the Stalin doctrine of Socialism in One

Country delivered body blows to the ideology of Free Trade. The Second World War disrupted whatever remained of free international trade. The production and exchange were entirely geared to the needs of the mighty war machines of the two coalitions engaged in a life and death combat. The end of Second World War and its aftermath saw the rapid extension of Communist rule in Eastern and Central Europe and the triumph of the Communist Revolution in China. This meant the withdrawal of a vast area of the earth from the already shattered international economy. Through the United Nations, GATT, World Bank, IMF and other agencies, the leading Western countries made half-hearted attempts to rebuild the World Economy on the basis of tariff reduction and free trade.

The newly freed countries like India, however, did not subscribe to the philosophy of liberalisation and insisted on protecting their nascent industries from competition by advanced nations, as Germany, the US and Japan had done years ago when they were in the early phase of industrialisation. But this protection was continued for too long and disabled our industries.

The emergence of the Soviet Union—with its planned economy—as a great military power also acted as a check on the process of globalisation of production and exchange.

But several new factors now intervened which powerfully aided the resumed advance of the process of globalisation. The spinx-like rise of Japan as a great industrial giant, and its nexus with the United States and the export-oriented economics of some other Asian countries helped in this process. Marx's other prediction about the division of society into two classes, the disappearance of the intermediate strata, pauperisation and the eventual overthrow of capitalism by its grave-digger—the proletariat—was however falsified.

The slowing down of economic growth in the USSR, the diversion of vast resources to defence, over-extension of its foreign military, economic and financial commitments were bound to take their toll. While the system of Centrally Planned Economy achieved spectacular results in the era of primitive industrialisation it was unable to cope with the demands of the Second Industrial (knowledge and information) Revolution. The Soviet philosophy had promised to the people an ever-increasing standard of living. The goal it had set up was to overtake the United States. But in the seventies and the early eighties the goal began increasingly to recede.

The revolution in communication destroyed the isolation of the Communist world. The Iron Curtain was no longer a feasible policy; it melted away. The falsity of the state propaganda about the material conditions in the West and the ideal state of affairs in the USSR was exposed. The Soviet people keenly and increasingly felt the gulf between promise and reality. They were dazzled by the material prosperity of the West and Japan.

The USSR had become a big importer of grain, an admission that its collectivised agriculture and network of state farms had failed to deliver the goods. In agriculture and industry, in the materials revolution, in the production of better substitutes, the USSR lagged behind the advanced countries and, what is more important, its people, brought upon the values of materialism, saw that it was lagging behind. The Soviet Union was using its oil and gold and diamonds to finance its imports of machinery and consumer goods. This was a return to a kind of colonial exchange—export of raw material and import of machinery and finished products. In these circumstances it was difficult even for the ruling elite of the USSR to believe that Soviet Communism was the wave of the future. *It is my belief that it was more the lure of Consumerism of the West than dissatisfaction with the absence of human rights and democracy in the USSR that brought about the disintegration of the Soviet system.*

The orthodox Communists have not learnt anything from the sudden and complete collapse of the Comecon—Warsaw Pact system. They continue to parrot old formulas: "The world is entering into a period of a fiercer struggle between the forces of imperialism and socialism in various spheres.... Changes in the international situation, of world capitalism and world socialism cannot lead to the conclusion that the fundamental contradictions of our epoch today stand modified.... the main assessment of the present epoch as that of a transition from capitalism to socialism on a world scale, which had started with the October Revolution, remains fully valid."[3] The hopes of India's Marxists now came to be centered on China, Vietnam and other surviving Communist one-party states.

But what is happening in China and Vietnam? The Chinese have opened their economy to the developed countries. These countries are not investing only or even chiefly in high technology areas. The United States is coming in with its full paraphernelia and its cultural symbols. Food processing is one their main targets.

Thus Coca Cola has recently entered the Chinese market in collaboration with its Chinese partners. It thinks that "China's potential is mind-boggling." Cadbury and Campbell also see limitless possibilities in the production of chocolates and soups in China.

The brave Vietnamese who fought the Japanese, the French and the Chinese successfully and made the Americans run for dear life have finally succumbed to the lure of the US culture and economy. Recent news reports are interesting: One day in February, two giant inflated Coca-Cola bottles appeared in the centre of Hanoi. It was just after the United States ended its 30-year trade embargo, and the symbolism could not have more apt: blatant American consumerism, resurrected at long lost and brazen as ever, was wasting no time establishing an offensive, even in the very capital of Vietnam's Communist heartland... Dinh, manager of SJC (concern) "holds 35% of the International Beverage Co. which began bottling Pepsi-Cola soft drink *only hours after* the US lifted its embargo..."[4]

Another story said: "Slick spots showing this year's Miss Vietnam sipping Pepsi Co's choice of a new generation' and pounding at a rock time on an electric key-board began airing on Vietnam's prime-time television a day after the United States lifted its trade embargo on Vietnam. Rival Coca-Cola says it will spend US $250,000 over the next ten days on its 'Glad to see you again' campaign featuring concerts, billboards and TV commercials which ran alongside of Pepsi's adds.[5]

To cap this all—as it were—the organ of the world's most orthodox Marxist Party—the CPI-M—not only did not protest the arrival of the supreme symbol of Americanism—Coca Cola—in the Metropolitan city of Calcutta, it virtually greeted its appearance by publishing a full-page coloured Coca-Cola advertisement. Can these gentlemen—no, comrades—be taken seriously when they rail against the Final Act?[6]

References

1. *The Economist*, 18 December, 1993.
2. *The Communist Manifesto*, Karl Marx and Fredrich Ergels.
3. *The CPI-M Central Committee Statement*, 28-31 May, 1990.
4. Far Eastern Economic Review, 31 March, 1994, pp. 62-63.
5. *Ibid*, p. 66.
6. *The Telegraph*, 30 March 1994.

8

A POLICY FOR INDIA IN A CRUEL WORLD

The debate on economic policy and the Uruguay negotiations has, I fear, an unreality which bodes ill for the country. The debaters have not taken sufficient note of two unpleasant developments and their impact on world politics and trade negotiations. The parties of the Right never evaluated properly the significance of the existence of the countervailing power of the Soviet Union and the protective umbrella it provided to the developing countries. The left-minded people too have ignored the long-term consequences of the disintegration of the Soviet Union and the system of political and economic alliances it had created.

Another development which the debaters, especially the advocates of the GATT agreement, forget is the hard fact that neither the United States, nor the European Union nor Japan has charity as the chief goal in multilateral trade negotiations. They are in business to promote their own interests. Whether the means adopted by them are appropriate or not—some wise economists think that they are misconceived—the fact is that they dispose superior technological, industrial and military might, and can force developing countries to fall in line with their prescriptions.

It is quite clear that we cannot pursue an isolationist policy. Nor can we insulate ourselves from the World Economy. Where Socialism in One Country failed—although the Soviet system embraced a far larger geographical area than India and possessed vaster natural resources it also failed—can we continue our Fortress India policy?

It was estimated that the number of households viewing Star TV rose from 4,800,000 in January 1993 to 30,506,000 in October 1993 in China as against India's increase from 3,300,000 in January 1993 to 7,278,000 in October 1993. What did the Chinese do? Alarmed by the rapid progress of the Western Cultural invasion and its economic fall-out, the one-party Chinese Communist state issued an order removing the dish antennas and restricting the access of international TV broadcasters and information networks. Saudi Arabia did the same thing to protect its Islamic "religious and social values."[1]

Can India really emulate these examples and suppress the foreign media and information flows? The thing is simply impossible to contemplate. With Technological advance even dish antenas would become unnecessary.[2]

A former Foreign Secretary has said that the Government of India played a passive role in trade negotiations and that it was negligent in mobilising the developing countries in order to resist the pressure of industrialised countries during the GATT negotiations.

In his evidence before the Standing Committee of Parliament, a former Foreign Secretary was quite critical of the handling of the negotiations by India. It is better to state the chargesheet in his own words: "What was our brief when I was one of the negotiators? Our brief was that we should not accept any norm or standards for IPR.... So far as the services sector is concerned, our brief was that not to liberalise and therefore, we will have to protect our services sector and we should seek to liberalise in labour services sector. So far as textiles are concerned, we should seek substantial liberalisation. The brief which we had till April, 1989, i.e. from December, 1986 to April, 1989, was altogether given up.... A Government's duty is to negotiate, do its best to extract maximum advantage. And my submission is that since the Dunkel draft was submitted, the Government has not made adequate and requisite effort to improve its position in the negotiations.... About Uruguay Round I can tell you, on the basis of my long experience with negotiations that our negotiations and participation in the Uruguay

Round has been a sad story of our extraordinary, inexplicable shyness and hesitance in trying to mobilize the developing countries. I would therefrom say that to a very great extent we ourselves, have been responsible for our isolation."[3]

Of course the witness conceded that India could not stay out of GATT negotiations. He said: "I think I would be trying to act very brave if I say that we can really stay out of the negotiations... But I would say that the responsibility for putting ourselves in this hopeless position is entirely that of the Government."[4]

A respected journalist has more or less made the same accusations. Perhaps he based himself on the former Foreign Secretary's evidence, I do not know. He charged the Government with "inertia and grovelling" and said that "barring the first phase there was an amazing passivity on the part of the Indian delegation at the GATT talks." But there is the other side of the coin. I shall therefore quote from the evidence of Anwar Hoda, Special Secretary, Commerce, before the Standing Committee. Hoda agrees with the ex-Foreign Secretary that their brief was to oppose inclusion of new issues such as Services, investments, and Intellectual Property Rights. The initiative in bringing up these issues as also the question of elimination of subsidies to agriculture was taken by the United States. *Hoda said that though India opposed inclusion of Intellectual Property Rights and Services, since "every country" was in agreement about opening negotiations on these, "we also agreed."*[5]

Now the Government spokesmen have not thrown any light on the reasons for the change in the attitude of developing countries nor on why the United States was keen on expanding the ambit of these trade negotiations. To my mind the answer is obvious and it lies in the big changes that had taken place in international politics. A Western economic journal provides a clue to the changed ethos at the GATT talks: "For decades, GATT has been the world's most successful forum for global co-operation... For many of those years, that looked like wishful thinking: much of the world was committed to a different ideology. The revolution of the late 1980s in the former Soviet Union promised to change this. With the socialist model in ruins, pro-market politicians made ground everywhere, especially in third world. *And this was an important reason* why the Uruguay round worked out as it did: the developing countries are keen as never before to liberalise trade and embrace market economics."[6]

In the better part of the eighties the United States and other industrialised countries were pursuing protectionist policies. But towards the end of the decade the US reversed its direction. The Soviet collapse opened the markets of Eastern Europe and the USSR. Besides, the US leaders now realised that while their trade deficit related to merchandise trade, the Services trade produced "a large surplus." They became aware that international Services trade was increasing and that the US had "the largest share" of this trade among developed countries.[7] The decline in the US farm exports induced the US representatives to introduce the issue of farm subsidies, the highest subsidisers being the European Union and Japan.

In addition the deteriorating economic conditions further undermined India's negotiating strength. The Leftists were already protesting against V.P. Singh Government's "indiscriminate liberalisation", its likely acceptance of the IMF World Bank conditionalities, galloping prices and so on. By the time the new Government assumed office, the country was on the verge of a terrible foreign exchange crisis. Even now stagnation in production, uncontrolled inflation and budgetary deficits are matters of deep concern.

It would, however, be valid criticism to say that the successive governments had failed to introduce competition and improve the public sector. But given the establishment's commitment to Consumerism—and this includes its ruling as well as opposition segments—there is no easy way out.

A person like me has never subscribed to the Liberal—Social Democratic—Communist goal of ever increasing standard of living. But I am conscious that only an insignificant minority shares my values and perception. The rising middle class is dying to enter the Consumers' Paradise. The TV watching poor also dream about the glittering prospect.

Apart from the various non-economic devices, the US actions can adversely affect India's security environment and increase its defence burdens by further arming Pakistan. India has to make the best of a bad job. The Foreign Policy set up needs to be reeducated. It must become more knowledgeable and more flexible. It must learn to give importance to trade, commerce and foreign economic policy. India must make shifting alliances to promote its national interests in an increasingly cruel and hostile world.

References

1. *The Asian Age*, Bombay, 2 March, 1994, and *The Hindu*, 12 March, 1994.
2. A recent report on China Said:
   Nobody came to take away Mr. Yang's dish antena. "So we just kept quiet", he said. The dish remains on his porch. It is not just individuals who are ignoring the dish ban, but Yang's state-run work units also. Whatever the policy, it will prove hard to keep broadcasts out of China. (*The Economist*, 2 July 1994).
3. *Department Related to Parliamentary Standing Committee on Commerce, (1993-94), Evidence*, pp. 31, 32 and 33.
4. *Ibid*, p. 33.
5. *Department Related to Parliamentary Standing Committee on Commerce (1993-94), Evidence*, pp. 3, 5, etc.
6. *The Economist*, December 18th 1993, p. 9.
7. *Foreign Affairs*, Volume 73, No. 1, p. 100.

9

SOCIALISTS : SELLING STALE BREAD

There was a time when Dr. Rammanohar Lohia used the production figures of steel and coal as a rough index of the level of economic development and also made higher targets for these items the centre of planned economic endeavour. The policy statement he prepared for the Allahabad Conference in 1953 gave pride of place to steel in the Socialist Party's governmental programme. It said:

> The Socialist Government will programme to increase the capacity for steel production by two million tones. With the current capacity 1.2 million tons, and assuming an increase to 2 million tons by the time socialism obtains power, the Socialist Government will raise India's steel capacity to four million tons just about what Japan currently produces. Compared with the giants of steel like the USA with its annual 110 million tons and the USSR with its 35 million tons, *as also with its own requirements appropriate to a decentralised economy*, India will be far behind, but the base for rapid progress thereafter will have been laid.[1]

But after economic development had passed a certain stage and had entered the era of diversification and sophistication, the use of these tests as the only or even the primary index of economic, industrial and technological power no longer remained valid. I doubt whether Lohia would have failed to take cognisance of the new developments, to revise his ideas, especially in the area of materials revolution and the breakthrough in the knowledge and information technology.

Lohia, it should be remembered, always laid stress on the development of human resource in order to transform the greatest drag on progress into an accelerator, on training, on invention and use of small unit technology—like desk top publishing—and creation of real wealth.

Lohia had a wide alert and open mind, and he kept himself abreast of developments in all walks of life around the globe. He related these developments to his principles and ideological outlook. He would use his theoretical formulations to appraise and evaluate these events, and the same time he would not hesitate to modify his own doctrinal positions in the light of changing reality. Unlike the Marxist theoreticians of the B.T. Ranadive variety, he did not twist the new facts or evidence to fit any preconceived theoretical framework. How many times I had heard him telling his followers not to sell stale bread; "*Basi roti mat becho,* replenish your stock of facts and ideas", he used to tell them.

Unfortunately most of Lohia's followers are adept in selling tattered garments. They repeat parrot like the slogans and ideas he advanced in the fifties and sixties or ideas even older than this. Lohia disliked people quoting something that Gandhi or Marx or anyone else, including himself, had said long ago. "Ask yourself this question, what was the context in which these remarks were made", he told his friends. Lohia always viewed any statements of ideas against their historical setting.

In 1965 on the invitation of the East Germans Lohia and I paid a visit to the German Democratic Republic, then held to be a model Soviet type economy. I had occasion to have several discussions with him on the comparative strength of the Soviet and Western economies. Lohia thought that the superiority of Western economic performance was self-evident, but he did not then detect the rot that had begun to set in the entire Soviet world. After the GDR visit I toured the Soviet Union. My request to visit Siberia was granted. I was shown the giant power project on the Angara river and was taken to a most modern pulp and chemical factory. The employees were all young men and women who enjoyed 25 per cent higher wages and salaries, and who used their spare time, including lunch hour, to prosecute higher scientific and mathematical studies. Eventually the chemical plant proved to be an ecological disaster for largest sweet water lake—Baikal. In this trip I also learnt about plants operating with pre-World War I machinery. The Soviet economy presented a contrast of the most modern factories existing side by side with those operating with the most obsolete equipment. But still industries of both types were operating within the parameters of the First Industrial Revolution.

However, in the Western World, especially the United States, Japan and Germany the perspectives were changing. A new revolution had silently begun without causing violent social and economic upheaval. The knowledge and information revolution had begun slowly and it would gather momentum in the next twenty years and profoundly transform the World Economy.

Lohia died in October 1967. His last definitive statement on the performance of the Western, Japanese and Communist economies is contained in his forty-seven page Preface to a collection of his essays entitled *Marx, Gandhi and Socialism*. Lohia's thinking was dominated by the Euro-American *versus* Asia and the Third World Divide, the contradiction which dominated all alert third world minds in the thirties despite the post-Second World War progress of decolonisation around the world, just as the thinking of the Europe's Communists was coloured by the experience of the Great Depression, the growing army of unemployed, the Soviet Union's astonishing planned progress and the conflict between the capitalists and the proletariat.

In the early sixties Lohia thought that in the world of relative phenomena, the superior achievements of North Korea and Cuba as against South Vietnam and Taiwan "must be recognised and analysed". Of course they were not comparable, he said, to anything achieved by Europe. Nevertheless he thought that Cuba was ahead of Taiwan on the issue of material achievements; the latter was "travelling on the energy road of innovation" whereas there was no such rousing in Taiwan.[2]

Lohia was so much under the influence of the conflict between the two giants that he neither saw nor anticipated the great changes in the global situation that would be unveiled after his death. Lohia did not think much of the progress achieved by Asian countries like China and India and others, for he thought that what was important was to measure this progress against that made by Euro-America—a concept in which he included the Soviet European bloc also. He generally tended to underplay the Japanese achievements. He wrote:

> On this view, the record is gloomy and the prospect is dismal. Japan is the first among Asians and it is only by courtesy that she may be called the last of Europeans and by right, not for a long time yet. The gap between Asians and Euro-Americans already big is further widening. Euro-American productivity is at least ten times the Asian and with every day the distance grows. That applies to guns as well as butter and Euro-American's superiority is unchallenged in either sphere. Nothing that the two of them, China and Marxism, have so far done has altered the picture even in a small way. Nor is a sign of a different future in evidence. The rate of growth in several mature countries of Europe is higher than in China. If the European rate tends sometimes to slacken as the maturity advances, the Chinese economy though still raw with vigour is exhibiting a similar up and down. There is no escape from Euro-American superiority, not at least with the Chinese model.[3]

Repeatedly Lohia told the Socialists and other leftists that socialism in India must be basically production-oriented and not distribution-oriented. He was not indifferent to equitable distribution. But he was totally opposed to the greed of organised workers and middle-class employees with their endless demands for wage and salary increases, holidays, and leaves of all kinds. He was for lowering wage differentials and rewarding more generously those who did arduous and dirty jobs—drainage workers, sweepers, miners and so on—or had to work under stress like the BEST's drivers and conductors operating in congested localities of the vast urban conurbation of Bombay. He also advocated this cause to break the linkage of dirty jobs and low caste status and take a giant step towards equality and social justice. Lohia did not believe in the endless pursuit of ever increasing wants;

his ideal was a decent standard of living. He powerfully raised the issue of India's poverty, and therefore always stressed hard work, limitation of consumption for a decade or so, building up of capital assets and productive apparatus through savings and investment and even voluntary labour—*ek ghanta desh ko.* He was not a supporter of collectivisation and ridiculed Nehru's bogus cooperativisation of agriculture. Nor was he dogmatic about bureaucratic nationalisation. It is a pity that some of his followers miss the essence of his teaching and relish selling stale bread.

References

1. *Marx, Gandhi and Socialism,* Rammanohar Lohia, 1978, p. 405.
2. *Ibid,* pp. x-xi.
3. *Ibid, 1978, p. vii.*

10

MARXISTS : WORSHIP OF OBSOLETE DOGMAS

At the high tide of the Brezhnev era (1964-83), the Soviet leaders used to exude unusual confidence about the prospects of Soviet economic development. They thought that they were on the verge of outstripping not only the old West European countries, but also the United States. Even in the earlier Khrushchev era the world's Communists were quite sanguine about their future. Their 1960 Statement had predicted the worldwide triumph of their system. The Statement said:

> It is the principal characteristic of our time that the world socialist system is becoming the decisive factor in the development of society.... The world capitalist system is going through an intense process of disintegration and decay.... Capitalism impedes more and more the use of the achievements of modern science and technology in the interests of social process... The time is not far off when socialism's share of world production will be greater than that of capitalism.... Today the restoration of capitalism has been made impossible not only in Soviet Union, but in the other socialist countries as well.

The Soviet leaders were wont to measure economic progress in terms of the gross output of iron ore, pig iron, steel, coal and oil. They thought that the most cogent index of a country's level of economic development was the amount of power it produced.

The USSR, the Soviet spokesmen exultantly said, had now surpassed the United States in the production of many important industrial goods: iron ore, coke, coal, ingot steel, non-ferreous metals, extraction of petroleum and production of mineral fertilisers. In the eyes of the Soviet leaders Japan was of no consequence, and its comparisons were all with the Western World, especially the United States. They proudly said that the USSR had been smelting more iron and steel than West Germany, Great Britain, France and Italy combined. "The Soviet industrial output had by 1970 reached upto three-quarters that of the US, and, by 1974, it had further gone up to four-fifths of the US figure."

But already by 1976 the Soviet criteria of treating output of coal, steel and oil, as the only—or even chief—indicator of economic strength were on the way to becoming dubious tests. Within a decade and half they became entirely irrelevant in assessing the strength of the top industrial powers.

The Russian Czarist Empire was once an exporter of grain. But Stalinist collectivisation completely destroyed Soviet agriculture. The United States with an insignificant portion of its population engaged in agriculture could not only feed itself, but also export its farm products on a large scale. The USSR had become a large importer of grain, year after year, although more than 30 per cent of its population was engaged in agriculture as against three to four per cent that of the United States.

The orthodox Marxists and those who proudly call themselves "unrepentent Communists" continued to hang on to the same old shibboleths, including the above criteria. They quoted with glee the Soviet Union's new records in coal, steel and oil output and its successful nuclear race with the United States. They hugged the theory of the escalating and even terminal crisis of capitalism, the growing pauperisation of the industrial workers under capitalism as also the key role of the blue collar proletariat as the harbinger of the new epoch.

To them a centrally planned economy, nationalisation of all major and medium industries, the strategy of controlling the commanding heights of the economy through an expanding public sector, and collectivisation or cooperativisation of agriculture were all sacred cows. The Indian Communists considered work ethics a mortal sin. The more holidays there were better was the lot of the workers and the nation; the more bandhs there were—*organised by the state and its ruling Marxist party*—no matter, whether on the flimsiest grounds, was a great thing, a reflection of the rising class consciousness!

Japan which today is the second biggest industrial power neither had any iron ore nor any metallurgical or other varieties of coal nor any petroleum resources. Thanks to the external constraints it could not develop nuclear power like France. It entirely depended on imports of these raw materials—iron ore, coal and oil. Japan was perpetually in dread of a sharp rise in the prices of these raw materials. The spectre finally gripped the Japanese with the oil shock of 1973 and the formation of the Opec cartel. But Japan had already fortified itself against this danger. In fact the preparations had begun in the sixties itself. The revolution in the science of materials, in the output of ever cheaper and more effective substitutes, such as fibre glass cables for copper cables, the perfection of the energy-saving devices and the great knowledge and information revolution enabled Japan to overcome the crisis. *Between 1965 to 1985, according to a reliable calculation, Japan was able to increase its industrial output by two and half times without increasing the 1965 level of its consumption of raw materials and oil.* This miraculous second revolution completely bypassed the USSR. In fact its leadership was not really not aware of its existence. It was also ignorant of the fact that by wastefully and recklessly using its vast raw material resources, including petroleum, and it's steel output it was crippling its potential strength and laying the basis for a deep economic crisis and eventual political collapse.

The Indian Communists, who pride themselves on being equipped by "the most scientific theory" and who unlike the Soviet functionaries had access to foreign documents, statements, monographs, journals, magazines and books, were also blissfully uninformed about these epoch-making developments. *I had a most revealing glimpse into the astonishing dogmatism and ignorance of the Marxist leaders in the Karl Marx Death Centenary Year (1983).* Comrade Shrinivas Sardesai wanted to hold a discussion on the relevance of Marxism and repeatedly asked me to participate in it. Despite my health problem, I finally agreed. The meeting was held at the Bombay University Club House. Among the speakers were

Dr. V.M. Dandekar, Usha Mehta, B.T. Ranadive and myself. I could see that Sardesai was upset by my outspoken analysis of the Soviet System. I offered a devastating criticism of the Soviet centralised planning, its bureaucratism, its huge outlay on defence, the colossal failure of its collectivised agriculture, its imports of large quantities of food grains, its stagnant economy and its failure to satisfy consumer needs. Then, I went on to dwell on the knowledge and information revolution and the revolution in the science of materials and substitutes which was sweeping Japan, Germany and the United States and said that the USSR planners were grossly wasting their vast resources. The Soviet Foreign Trade had assumed the character of colonial exchange, the Soviets providing oil and raw materials and importing manufactured goods and machinery. On this note I ended my speech. S.G. Sardesai, at this point, quite discourteously, asked B.T. Ranadive not only to speak but to refute the criticism advanced by us—the reformist critics of Marxism-Leninism—and said that he could take as much time as he needed. Comrade Ranadive made a tub-thumping speech dismissing all my arguments with contempt and grandly predicting the global victory of Marxism-Leninism. I was flabbergasted by the obtuseness of the biggest Marxist-Leninist theoretician of the Indian Communist Movement. But Ranadive was a fine man, devoted and, unlike S.A. Dange, a practitioner of Gandhian simplicity. When he was on his death bed I visited him. He talked of the decline of values, of idealism, and so on, and therefore when I left him, a piercing sadness benumbed me. Unfortunately—or rather fortunately—Ranadive died *a few weeks later* and did not have to witness the total disintegration of the Soviet system, China's opening of its economy to the West, its culture, including Coca-Cola, and its earnest bid to get into the Gatt again.

It pains me greatly that the cataclysmic changes of the last ten years have not made any impact on the Communists and the Marxists here. I carefully went through all their recent publications and I was surprised to find that they reaffirmed their belief in the so called "four basic contradictions". Dictatorship of the Proletariat, leading role of the party, democratic centralism and nationalization of the major means of production and centralized planning. It shows their dogged refusal to re-examine *their own doctrines*. And yet the world is flying away from their dogmas with the speed of light. The result is the growing divergence between their profession and their practice. Really speaking there is no recognizable difference between the quality of their administration and the flavour of the governance of other parties. The Marxist party also has a nexus with the Mafiosi, it is not above rigging polls and it has no compunction about hobnobbing with minority communalism of different varieties—they consider only majority communalism to be dangerous—and particularly making covert and overt alliances with the Muslim fundamentalists in Kerala. It is really ironical that a movement claiming to possess not only an all-India perspective but a world outlook should be confined to two corners of India—eastern and southwestern. I have lost all hope that the Marxists will ever turn their searchlights inwards. The Communists will never replenish their stock of ideas, for alas! they continue to worship their rusted and obsolete dogmas.

11

ANTI-GATT FRONT : A NON-STARTER

There was a little noticed meeting in Delhi in April 1994, of which the sponsors were some senior journalists like Prabhash Joshi of *Janasatta* and Nikhil Chakravarty of *Mainstream*, social scientists like Rajani Kothari, and the former justice of Supreme Court, Krishna Iyer. The meeting was held on 13 April 1994 and its main object was to build up a broadbased front against the Gatt Final Act. Another meeting was to take place on 10 May 1994. Among those who expounded their views were S.P. Shukla and George Fernandes.

The list of participants is not without significance. No Congressmen was present, and so the meeting could be construed as an attempt to revive and reconstruct a non-Congress Front, this time on the Gatt issue: George Fernandes and Jaipal Reddy (Janata Dal); Nirmal Kanti Chatterjee (CPI-M); Geeta Mukerjee and Bhogendra Jha (CPI); K.C. Sudershan (General Secretary of the RSS); Murlidhar Rao (Swadeshi Jagaran Manch of the RSS); Mahesh Sharma (of the Deendayal Shodha Sansthana), Rajendra Sachar (of the PUCL); Shanti Bhushan (former Law Minister of the Janata Party Government), Ashoka Panda and Swami Agnivesh (who is going to float a new party of which the main plank would be that religion and politics cannot be separated).

If the statement attributed to N.K. Chatterjee of the CPI-M by the Special Correspondent of *Janasatta* is believable, he is said to have claimed that a united front is necessary and that there should be no difficulty about rising above their ideological differences for this purpose. Jaipal Reddy sought a united front in the Rajya Sabha to defeat the amendment to the Patent Act.[1]

I cannot vouchsafe for the veracity of this report. But we know this much that nothing came out of these confabulations. Nor is this very surprising. The idea of some people (belonging to the Sangh Pariwar) was to revive the JP movement of 8 April 1974. The idea is a sign of immaturity. History does not repeat itself. And if it did, it would be in the shape of a farce or worse as Karl Marx once said.

Some of the participants have absolutely no capacity for mass mobilisation. But they are pleased to see their names in the print media and even more pleased if their faces appear on the T.V. Screen. Some are downright gullible and some are confirmed hypocrites. My friends Chandra Shekhar and George Fernandes, who feel strongly about Gatt—rightly or wrongly—are the most sincere about organising united resistance to the Final Act and what it means.

George Fernandes attended a meeting in Bombay in which Gopinath Mundhe, leader of the BJP's Legislative Wing in Maharashtra also took part. George's Party members did not approve his action. Then he tried to bring together amorphous leftist groups, including the IPF. But the leader of this group, Vinod Mishra, in his speech told George bluntly that unless the Sangh Pariwar apologises for its 6 December 1993 act of vandalism, he would not even consider making common cause with them.

The Sangh Pariwar was never serious about its opposition to the PVNR's Government's economic policy. In his speech on the General Budget on 29 July 1991 the BJP spokesman Jaswant Singh referred to the Central Government's Industrial Policy statement and said that the BJP had considered it and went along with "the broad thrusts" of that policy.[2]

Next year A.B. Vajpayee supported globalisation in his Budget oration and said that it was true that they could *not* "remain isolated in today's world".[3] L.K. Advani, Leader of the Opposition, donned the mantle of the unofficial Ambassador at large and canvassed support for the Government's liberalisation policy.

The BJP has of late drawn a distinction between globalisation and *internal liberalisation*. This is a bogus distinction. If you abolish licencing and introduce real competition what would happen? Let us assume that four enterprising industrialists come forward to start new automobile manufacturing units. What will they do? One would seek cooperation with, say, America's Ford Motor Company. The second one will desire a link up with Japan's Toyota. A third one may consider a connection with Germany's BMW, which has recently taken over Britain's Rover, more useful. And the last one—the fourth aspirant—may think collaboration with a French manufacturer more rewarding. They will all need large investments and import of the plant and machinery which cannot be fabricated here. This will require huge amounts of foreign exchange. Advani's Sangh Pariwar cannot come to the rescue of the would be manufacturers of cars. They will have to look to the industrialised countries. That is why internal liberalisation and globalisation are inseparable. Only stupid fools will fail to perceive the connection. The Japanese once did the trick of importing lavishly new technology and adapting it without importing Western capital except in the infrastructure area. *But they could do this because for decades they curbed consumption, encouraged savings and turned savings into productive investment.*

The BJP's important electoral segment is the urban middle class. It is consumerist to the core. It indulges in share transactions to get rich quick. The Japanese were given income tax reliefs—the exemption limit was deliberately kept low—if they invested in Post Office Savings Schemes *with ridiculously low* interest rates, yes not even half of what India's nationalised banks are giving on time deposits after the latest Reserve Bank directives. The pronouncement of the RSS Chief that the anti-Gatt agitation cannot be our chief plank and Govindacharya's comic statement at a recent Ramlila Maidan rally that "we want to carry on the anti-Gatt struggle without getting bruised," what do these show? Has there been any real struggle—even a not-violent one—without sustaining bruises? But the statement coming as it does from the member of a Pariwar which specialised in sending apology letters during the Emergency should not surprise anybody.

The Marxists are no less hypocritical than the BJP. Jyoti Basu admits that after liberalisation investers have begun to show interest in West Bengal. He wants the multi-nationals to come. *Ganashakti's* full page coloured Coca-Cola advertisement was symbolic of their real policy. How can the Marxists fail to fall in line with China and Vietnam?

I am glad my friend George Fernandes's eyes have begun to see the reality. Recently, this advocate of all-out cooperation with the Sangh Pariwar said at Dhanbad: "We should not set up a trap for ourselves, then walk into it, like for instance the BJP is doing." He accused the BJP of "double speak" on the Dunkel question. Pointing to the BJP's support for the new economic policy, he described the BJP's position as "hypocritical and self-deceptive", and added that this "can only encourage the Government and also the transnationals which can see through the shadow-boxing."[4]

Even in the case of Chandra Shekhar, who embarked upon a nationwide campaign, appealing to "all patriotic forces including the RSS to come together", the disillusionment has set in. In the midst of the campaign, he openly accused the BJP of lacking "seriousness" on the issue. More importantly, Chandra Shekhar hastened to add a rider to his joint campaign idea by demanding from the Sangh Pariwar "suspension of its Hindutwa campaign."

How long this moment of clarity will last in my friends' restless souls, I cannot say. *But sooner they realise that transnational company is the specific form of business organisation in this age, and advise all dynamic Indian private and public sector companies to go transnational themselves, the better it will be for the national economy.*

References

1. *Janasatta*, 14 April 1994.
2. *Lok Sabha Debates*, 29 July, 1991.
3. *Lok Sabha Debates*, 23 March 1992.
4. *The Hindu*, 28 May 1994.

12

WORK ETHOS AND DEVELOPMENT

One need not accept of Mahatma Gandhi's views on "physical labour and machines". Even in his scheme of things simple machines like a bicycle, *charkha* and sewing machines had a place. But his stress on hard work and absolute avoidance of wastage and pilferage of public money is a pre-condition of our material and moral progress.

Mahatma Gandhi worked very hard and did not waste a moment. He worked hard on things he considered important. In his philosophy of life, physical labour had an important place. Jawaharlal also worked very hard, and in the pre-freedom days plied his *charkha* quite often. But his activity was chiefly intellectual, and physical labour was not central to his thinking. On 6 February 1947—barely a year before his assassination—Gandhi wrote: "Intellectual work is important and has an undoubted place in the scheme of life. But what I insist on is the necessity of physical labour. No man, I claim, ought to be free from that obligation .... In this connection I would refer to the life of Tolstoy and how he made famous the theory of bread-labour first propounded in his country by the Russian peasant Bondaref."[1]

Whatever your differences with Gandhi and Tolstoy, there is no gain saying the fact that there a close connection between work culture and economic well-being. *To work hard does not, however, mean to work stupidly. It means to work smartly, expending minimum time and energy to do a specific job.* It does not necessarily mean physical labour, but does involve soiling your hands whenever required.

The system of "modern education" which the British introduced in India, with its emphasis on the Humanities and the study of languages—and only a bit of science—agreed perfectly with our anti-utilitarian old Brahmanical system and, in fact, the new system strengthened the old prejudices against labour, tools and techniques. The Brahmanical system had an innate contempt for work involving physical labour or work which meant soiling one's hands.

Our primary, middle and high school education did not have a technical bias. Exactly opposite was the state of affairs in the German or Japanese or American school systems. Recently *The Economist* wrote: "Historically, Britain has been good at educating the best. Trinity College, Cambridge, has produced more Nobel prize winners than many European countries. *Even at its best, British education has been infused with an anti-utilitarian, anti-commercial bias.* Cambridge first deigned to offer an MBA in 1991—83 years after Harvard and 65 years after Stanford. Oxford will offer one in 1996." But Britain's real historical weakness, the journal said, has been in its education of the masses (though things are improving with national vocational qualifications, a new apprenticeship scheme, and Training and Enterprize Councils).[2]

Max Weber's concept of protestant ethic and spirit of Capitalism was opposed to traditionalism, old customs and methods; it meant a rationalistic ethos. *Weber's spirit of capitalism, therefore, was actually the new and necessary work ethos, and not just acquisitive greed or single-minded pursuit of pecuriary gain, a meaning which came to be attached to the Weberian concept in later years. What Weber intended to signify by the concept "spirit of capitalism" was "working to the fullest possible capacity" of an individual, whether entrepreneur or worker.* This new ethos helped modernisation of the economy, growth of production and increase in productivity.[3]

But for the Indian Marxists work ethic is an anathema. In a recent article entitled *Deng Xiaoping and China's Reforms* on the gradual creation of a Chinese market economy, I found recurring references to the hard work put up by the Chinese in achieving an economic break through and the need for even harder work in the years to come. "We must work very hard. Our task is heavy and our responsibility is great," the important Chinese researchist concluded. I was not surprised. But our trade unionists here have destroyed work ethos in the public sector, central and State governments, panchayat and municipal services and even private industry. We had state sponsored Bandhs for seventeen years in West Bengal. This time Jyoti Basu put his foot down. But "the gap" was quickly filled by Tamilnadu's Chief Minister, Jayalalitha. The Government officers and employees do not work; they only want holidays. They loot the state and the public with great relish. They have not only bankrupted the Electricity Boards but several undertakings through their corruption and limitless avarice.

Recently I was talking to a big official of a reputed non-governmental research institute. I asked him about the work ethos in his institution. He said they were very strict, but the general ambience of permissiveness, lack of discipline and reluctance to work hard was affecting them also.

I also spoke to some officials and employees of the Central Government and institutions, wholly funded by it, about the effective working days. They said the situation was worse in the Government offices and these institutions than private firms.

The below mentioned table of the Central Government holidays and other leave benefits enjoyed by these employees is interesting:

Saturdays-Sundays	:	104 days
Yearly paid leave (i.e. earned leave)	:	30 days
Yearly half paid leave on medical grounds, etc.	:	20 days or 10 days full pay leave
Casual leave	:	12 days
Public Holidays	:	16 days
Restricted Holidays	:	2 days
TOTAL:-		174 days and
Maternity leave for women:		90 days

About the last item, I do not mind increasing the maternity leave by 10 days in the case of women who practise family planning and agree to have only one issue.

The above sum of non-working days does not include the holidays declared on the occasion of the death, natural or otherwise, of persons in high offices of the state.

There are at least two or three or more extended weekends in Delhi every year, when everything is closed, including the Parliament and its Library as also the Nehru Memorial Museum and Library. In fact the latter closes its facilities to research workers and scholars whenever functions attended by High Dignitaries are held there. And these occasions are not few. I find closure of institutions of research and libraries for days on end, especially, irritating. Nowhere in the world do the government and the elite make such a virtue out of sloth as in this country and show such contempt for work ethos.

It is no use citing the leave with pay enjoyed by the peoples of the industrialised world. For it cannot be forgotten that these countries have reached their present affluence after a century of long hours and hard work without the present benefits.

It is tragic that in this land of low productivity and low production, while *a minority of the work force is overworked,* the rest are allowed to pass away their time in idleness at Government expense. The worst case is that of teachers, from the primary level to the University level. They don't teach, or do research work: they only pocket the salaries and fellowship money. The existence of an honourable minority only proves the general prevalance of malingering and avoidance of work.

My friends are worried about the penetration of foreign banks. They speak of the three big Japanese banks whose assets each are over 15 lakh crores of rupees, almost a third of India's GDP. What Indian bank can compete with these banks, or American banks for that matter, they rhetorically asked. But none of these banks began with these mighty assets. It was Japan's economic policies which let them to grow big. Why Indian citizens are responding to overtures from foreign banks and have started opening their accounts in them? Because the trade unions (or employees) and associations (or officers) of our nationalised credit institutions hold that they are entitled to provide their customers *rotten service.* I am not unaware of the difficulties of the employees and faults of the top management. But the bankmen at all levels must realise that it is the people who put their money in the banks; and yet they are treated like beggers or worse. For cashing or depositing their cheques or getting their pass books for inspection or for depositing cash into their accounts or obtaining their time deposit certificates they have to visit the banks three or even five times. This is of course not my personal experience. Personally bank people have always treated me with great courtesy. But I am not dealing here with a personal problem; my experience is not the general experience of ordinary people. I don't see any sign of introspection on the part of trade union leaders about the miserable plight of these ordinary citizens. Did we support nationalisation for this purpose? Did we not do so because we thought they would help marginal and medium farmers, artisans and other self-employed persons?

The Governments in the States have become so big that the salaries, D.A.s and perquisites of the officers and employees and other administrative overheads surpass greatly the tax revenues. How can there be any real development?

Our Trade Unions have thus out-Bompersed the American trade Union leader Samuel Bompers who always asked for "More". The only difference is that our trade unions are doing this on the basis of low average national productivity. A time is not far off when the employees and workers in the organised sector, including the governments at all levels, will come forward with the demand that the Government and the employers fix only working days, say at 100, the rest being treated as holidays. In brief, it will be all play, no work, a free breakfast and also a free lunch all the year round. The top managers and executives excel the workers and employees in demanding and extorting from the firms fabulous perquisites. The list and the total amounts are mind boggling. The workers follow suit. In the wake of globalisation they would now both demand American incomes.

I recall the age of my childhood and youth. The working class then was a really exploited class. Now they have joined the ranks of the privileged. And yet whenever the agriculturists demand an increase in support prices or free movement or the right to export, the urban middle class sheds crocodile tears over the adverse impact of these demands on the poor of the land. *An inspection of productive farms in the country or the modern vineyards in Nasik and South Maharashtra would show how hard the small and medium farmers as well as agricultural labourers work.* They have no fixed hours and no 174 holidays in a year. The Government officers and employees and the Executives and workers in the orgaised sector never ponder over the effect of their salaries, D.A.s, perquisites and endless holidays on the level of prices. This does not bother the Marxists who hang on to their doctrine about the vanguard role of this "proletariat". The unfortunate fact is that no party wants to inaugurate a new age of simplicity, hard work and rapid increase in production to lift the country from the mire of poverty. *A real Social Security system, we must remember, can be built only on the basis of high productivity.*

References

1. *The Collected Works of Mahatma Gandhi,* Vol. 86, pp.436-37.
2. *The Economist,* 28 May 1994.
3. Otsuka Hisao, *Max Weber on the Spirit of Capitalism,* (A Symposium), Tokyo, 1985, p.86.

13

MUST COMPETITION BREED CONCENTRATION?

The signing of the Gatt Final Act and the question of India's relation with the new World or Multilateral Trade Organization, as it will be called, cannot be discussed in a vacuum. It has to be viewed against the background of the present international situation, the condition of our national economy and the relation of political forces in the country.

It should be remembered that all the forecasts made by even the most exceptionally gifted and far sighted men and women cannot come true. Karl Marx was one such gifted person. At a very young age he discerned the chief tendency of the future, which was not visible to lesser minds. In the Manifesto of the Communist Party, published "a few weeks before" the February 1848 Revolution, in France, the young Marx spoke, almost in a tone of exaltation, about the dynamic and rapidly expanding character of the bourgeois mode of production (the terms capitalism and capitalists were then not much in vogue) which had led to the establishment of what he already called "the world market". He wrote about the interaction of the growing productive forces and the voyages of discovery, developments in navigation, communications, commerce, joint stock companies and so on. He ridiculed the concept of national seclusion and self-sufficiency, and linked the "cosmopolitan character" of the production with "the universal inter-dependence of nations."[1]

When Marx published the first Volume of *Capital* in German almost two decades later (1867) he did not basically depart from the main formulations of the Manifesto. In a famous passage on concentration and centralisation in Chapter XXXII of Capital I, he wrote:

> That which is now to be expropriated is no longer the labourer working for himself, but the capitalist exploiting many labourers. This expropriation is accomplished by the action of the immanent laws of capitalistic production itself, by the centralisation of capital. *One capitalist always kills many. Hand in hand with this centralisation, or this expropriation of many capitalists by few,* develop, on an ever extending scale, the cooperative form of the labour process, the conscious technical application of science, the methodical cultivation of the soil, the transformation of the instruments of labour into instruments of labour only usable in common, the economising of all means of production by their use as the means of production of combined, socialised labour, *the entanglement of all peoples in the net of the world market, and with this, the international character of the capitalistic regime.* Along with the constantly diminishing number of the magnates of capital, who usurp and monopolise all advantages of this process of transformation, grows the mass of misery, oppression, slavery, degradation, exploitation; but with this too grows the revolt of the working-class, a class always increasing in numbers and disciplined, united, organised by the very mechanism of the process of capitalist production itself. The monopoly of capital becomes a fetter upon the mode of production, which has sprung up and flourished along with, and under it. Centralisation of the means of production and socialisation of labour at last reach a point where they become incompatible with their capitalist integument. Thus integument is burst asunder. The knell of capitalist private property sounds. The expropriators are expropriated.[2]

It will be seen that one of Marx's chief prediction that the explosive growth of the productive forces would tear asunder "the integument of the bourgeois relations of production" was falsified. In fact it was the new relations of production created by the Soviet Union and the Comecon countries based on the state ownership of the means of production which *choked* the growth of productive forces. Not only this; the irresistible attraction of consumerist capitalism of the West and the widespread popular disenchantment with the Communist one-party rule destroyed the Soviet system itself.

This happened because Marx's use of terms like relations of production, productive forces, mode of production and so on caused confusion. The Marxists neither analysed the interrelationship between what Marx called the productive forces and production relations nor carefully investigated the successive changes in the relations of production in the capitalist world.

On the question of concentration and centralisation, on monopoly *versus* competition, a lot of confusion has prevailed among the Marxists. Karl Kautsky held that "monopoly capitalism" and "competitive economy" were a contradition in terms. He thought that the process of monopolisation in capitalist society would eliminate competition altogether. Another Marxist school held that while "monopoly capitalism" would destroy competition within individual capitalist countries, it would assume the form of fierce competition and anti-imperialist rivalries among different capitalist powers whose national economies would become monopolistic in character.

It is not only the followers of Karl Marx who believed in the theory that free market and competition would lead to concentration and concentration would, eventually, produce an economy dominated by a few "monopolistic firms". This theory was subscribed to even by economists and business analysts of unimpeachable "bourgeosis" credentials, to use the expression current in young Marx time.

In the mid-fifties—to be precise, in 1956—the *Harward Business Reivew* took note of the new computer technology which had begun to emerge in the United States, and hazarded a prediction on its likely impact on the American economy. *The Harwc d Business Review* thought that the new invention of computer would lead to unprecedented concentration of American business within the next two or three decades. "The economy would be dominated by a few giant firms. Within each firm important decisions would be made by a handful of executives with access to the firm's single, big computer."

Many books appeared in the fifties and sixties which sounded the death knell of the medium size and small firms. A fearful picture of absolute concentration of capital and production was drawn by these writers. The thinking represented by *The Harvard Business Review* "boiled down to the idea that information technology would increase centralisation" of the decision making process by enabling the top managers to keep better track of information and enable this top personnel "to make wiser decisions and to disseminate them more widely."[3]

However the knowledge and information revolution took a curious turn and instead of promoting the type of absolute concentration visualised by the *The Harward Business Review* began to give a fillip to new small and medium size entrepreneurs and firms. The battle of Apple versus IBM was on when I visited America in the early eighties. The creation of a real world market, the erosion of regulated economies, lowering of trade barriers, new consumer demands were all supposed to help the further growth of the mighty firm. But an exactly contrary thing has happened. Even the organization and personnel of the down town or inner city offices of big firms is getting dispersed. With sophisticated personal computers and Fax and other facilities many executives and employees prefer to avoid daily commutation to the down town offices and operate from their homes. Not only efficiency has not suffered but other benefits have resulted as by-products of this process.

One of the main arguments of the crusaders against the Gatt Final Act was that Indian business firms, both public and private sectors, are too puny compared to General Motors, Toyota and so on, and would not be able to compete with them and would either shut down or become distributing agencies of the multi-nationals. But there is no need to quake and kowtow to giant firms. What is important is innovation, smartness and ability to foresee market trends.

A famous journal wrote not long ago: "Corporate giants once walked tall and proud, bestriding the globe, champions of this century's miraculous economic growth. The goal of every ambitious company was to join them and, like them, be mighty enough to shrug off the blows which regularly toppled smaller rivals. But these are troubling times for the world's biggest companies. Their presumption of invincibility is now in shreds. Spectacular failures at General Motors, IBM and Philips,once paragons of business success, have shown big firms to be frighteningly vulnerable to changes in their markets and to economic down turns. Hundreds of other big firms, from Japan's Matsushita to Germany's Daimler-Benz, are struggling to refashion themselves to avoid a similar fate. The humbling of big firms has only just begun. Economic recovery will offer some respite, but not much. In a broad range of industries, powerful forces are moving against big companies."[4]

Fierce competition allows innovaters to beat the large firms which rest on their laurels. According to Dataquest, a Houston-based firm, called Compaq Computer, had recently pushed aside IBM and also Apple Computer and become the world's largest personal computer (pc) maker. Its share of the world market *by volume* has risen to 9.5 per cent. What is the lesson? The giants can regain their strength only if they become effecient innovativeand "lean."[5]

To give only one example of how personal computers are going to affect business. Take the composing and printing business and book trade. You can now compose a complete book at home, including page making on your P.S. Only the printing and *binding* has to be done outside.

Here in India our notions of monopoly have been quite hazy. Far from applying the term chiefly to the total market share of an individual enterprize, we introduced into it all sorts of notions about total assets, total turn-over and so on. In a way we were paranoic about big companies, high production and huge turnovers. Instead of introducing progressive delicencing and stimulating competition in a phased but deliberate manner, so that no private sector company was allowed to have a market share of 40 to 50 per cent, we put on their productive capacity all manner of crippling restrictions. *The employers were engaged here not in reducing cost of production and improving quality, but in lobbying in the Capital City of Delhi with a view to keeping their rivals out.* In the Janata Party Manifesto we had demarcated the area of small scale and cottage industries. We should have *enforced it through legislation* and opened other sectors to competition through delicencing as well as by lowering the tariff barriers. In a protected market the allround growth of the companies was stunted, technological innovation was discouraged, quality was neglected and consumer interests totally sacrificed. The Indian goods have earned a bad name here and abroad—as the Japanese had done in the thirties—and the craze for imported foreign-made products amongst our people, who once extolled *Swadeshi* in the broad sense, including the pioneering work of J. Tata, has crossed all limits. But that need not dishearten our dynamic entrepreneurs. As the revealing experience of the industrialised countries cited above shows, what counts is innovation and insight. What Apple did, they can also do. We are responsible for our own miserable condition, for not developing our vast human resources. We failed to abolish illiteracy, and make the people *employable by imparting them the necessary skills* as Germany and Japan had done. It is no use our blaming the IMF, World Bank, Gatt or the new WTO.

References

1. Karl Marx and Frederich Engels *Selected Works*,(Third Printing, Moscow, 1975), pp. 31, 37 and 39.
2. Karl Marx, *Capital I, Historical Tendency of Capitalist Accumulation*, Chapter XXXII, pp. 714-715.
3. *The Economist*, 15 December, 1990.
4. *The Economist*, April 17, 1993.
5. *The Economist*, 2 July 199; and 11 June 1994.

Section III

CONSTITUTIONAL AND PARLIAMENTARY CONTROVERSIES

14

WHO KILLED THE UNANIMOUS JPC REPORT?

In the year 1992 when the country was passing through a grave foreign exchange crisis and had initiated important policy changes in the direction of the liberalisation of the economy, a stock market scandal of enormous magnitude hit the unsuspecting people. The Finance Minister, Dr. Manmohan Singh, spoke of "the systems failure" and promised that the Government would try "to tone up the system". An enquiry under R. Janakiraman's "overall supervision" was to be conducted into the stock market operations, the functioning of the banking system and so on. These assurances given in March-April 1992 did not satisfy the Parliament or the people. To allay the widespread anxiety and the fears the Prime Minister P.V. Narasimha Rao made a statement on 9 July 1992 which *inter alia* said:

> I feel that there is need for a comprehensive inquiry through the instrument of Parliament which not only fully establishes Parliamentary Supremacy but also provides an effective safeguard to protect the country's interests. I am therefore requesting the Hon'ble Speaker to proceed with the formation of Parliamentary Committee and entrust it with the task.... I would like to assure this august House that my desire and purpose remain, as they have been so far, to unveil the truth and ensure the smooth transformation to a vibrant economy in the larger interest of the nation.[1]

It is a matter of deep regret that inspite of the fact that the initiative for an inquiry into the Stock Market Scam by a Committee of Parliament came from the Prime Minister, Congress spokesmen continued to attack the institution of inquiry by Parliamentary Committees and poured ridicule on its deliberations. No words of condemnation strong enough can be found to describe this reprehensible action.

The Committees of Parliament are of different kind. Some Committees are permanent Committees. Some Committees are *ad hoc* in nature. They are either set up to consider specific legislation, or to inquire into special subjects under parliamentary motions. It is not as if an *ad hoc* Committee of Parliament was proposed to inquire into a specific matter of public importance in August 1992 for the first time in the history of parliamentary democracy in our country. There have been several instances of such Committees being set up in the past. These Committees have achieved varying degrees of success. While some served the purpose well, some others have been disastrous, the result depending on the level of cooperation between the Ruling Party and the Opposition. The effectiveness of the probe—whether by a Parliamentary Committee or a Commission of Inquiry—is directly related to the real intention of the Government. Does it wish to ferret out the truth, improve the functioning of the institutions and punish the guilty or does it want to kill time and do a whitewashing job? A few instances would illustrate my point.

The first Committee to probe "the Conduct of a Member of Parliament" was set up on 8 June 1951. The Constitution had then come into force, but elections to Parliament and the State Legislatures had not taken place yet. It was the Provisional Parliament which was then functioning as the Union Legislature. The Committee consisted of T.T. Krishnamachari, K.T. Shah, Syed Nausherali, Durgabai and Kashinathrao Vaidya. TTK acted as Chairman.

The charge against Mudgal was that he had agreed to canvass support and make propaganda in their behalf in Parliament on a payment of Rs. 20000 by the Bombay Bullian Association. When the Prime Minister received information about this matter, he confronted Mudgal personally. Mudgal, however, denied the allegation. It was, therefore, decided to hold a probe into the allegation by a Committee of Parliament. The Committee called 24 witnesses. H.G. Mudgal was allowed to be represented by Counsel. The Attorney General himself opened the proceedings.

The Committee was satisfied that Mudgal had agreed "to render services" to the Bombay Bullion Association "in return for consideration". In actual fact only a small payment of Rs. 2000/- had been made in two instalments to Mudgal upto that time by the Association before the matter of bribe surfaced. The Committee noted, however, that Mudgal entertained "great expectations from this source". The Committee was unable to accept the explanation offered by Mudgal. It felt that the Member had withheld "material facts" from the Prime Minister and Parliament. The Committee did not comment on the ethics of the Bombay Bullion Association in making this offer to a Member of Parliament, but dismissed its attempt to make a distinction between H.G. Mudgal Publications and Mudgal as individual and Member of Parliament. The Committee held that Mudgal's conduct was "derogatory to the dignity" of Parliament and "inconsistent with the standards" which Parliament "is entitled to expect from its Members." The Report was submitted on 25 July 1951. H.G. Mudgal quickly resigned his seat, and no further action was taken on the Report.[2]

Now I shall take up a matter of far greater significance than the Mudgal Case. It involved a crore of rupees—a large sum in that age of innocence. The Mundhra Case (1957) raised important issues involving the ambit of powers of autonomous credit institutions, the role of the civil servants and, above all, of Ministerial responsibility to Parliament.

The classic statement of the doctrine of Ministerial responsibility to Parliament has been formulated by the Labour Party leader, Herbet Morrison. It cannot be improved upon. I will, therefore, give here a summary of this statement in his own words as far as possible.

One of the fundamentals of our system of government is that some Minister of the Crown is responsible to Parliament, and through Parliament to the public, for every act of the Executive. It has to be the Minister, for it is he, and neither Parliament nor the public, who has official control over his civil servants. This is a corner-stone of our system of parliamentary government. There may, however, be an occasion on which so serious a mistake has been made that the Minister must explain the circumstances and processes which resulted in the mistake.

Now and again the House demands to know the name of the officer responsible for the occurrence. The proper answer of the Minister is that if the House wants anybody's head it must be his head as the responsible Minister, and that it must leave him to deal with the officer concerned in the Department. In all these matters it is well for the Minister to be forthcoming in Parliament. *The House of Commons is generous to a Minister who has told the truth, admitted a mistake, and apologized; but it will come down hard on a Minister who* takes the line that he will defend himself and his Department whether they are right or wrong or who *shuffles about evasively rather than admit that a blunder* or an innocent mistake has been made.[3]

Not long after the publication of Morrison's book, the purchase by the nationalised LIC of the shares of the Mundhra Companies attracted wide "critical public attention" in 1957. The matter was first raised in the form of a question by Dr. Ram Subhag Singh. But the question was based on incomplete information and as usual an evasive answer was returned. Another precise question forced the Ministry to reveal the full facts. A debate was raised by Feroze Gandhi, who demanded a parliamentary probe into the scandal. The Prime Minister, however, preferred a Commission of Inquiry and Chief Justice M.C. Chagla was asked to investigate the matter. After weighing all the evidence Chagla delineated the areas of the responsibility of the Principal Secretary of the Ministry, H.M. Patel, and the Cabinet Minister, T.T. Krishnamachari. In Chagla's opinion, constitutionally the Minister was responsible for the action taken by his Secretary with regard to this transaction. It was clear that a Minister must take the responsibility for actions done by his subordinates. He could not take shelter behind them, nor could he disown their actions. The doctrine of ministerial responsibility had two facets. The Minister had complete autonomy within his sphere of authority. As a necessary corollary he was required to take full responsibility for the actions of his servants. It is true that this might throw a very great burden on the Minister because it was impossible to expect that in a highly complicated system of administration which we have evolved the Minister could possibly know, leave alone give his consent to, every action taken by his subordinates. But it was assumed that once the policy was laid down by the Minister, his subordinates would reflect that policy and would loyally carry out that policy. If any subordinate failed to do so, he might be punished or dismissed, but, however, vicariously, the responsibility of his action had to be assumed by the Minister. It could be said that a Minister was merely part of the Government and his policy was the policy of the Government as a whole, and if the Minister should take the responsibility for his subordinate's actions, equally so must the Cabinet. But it was well established that the Cabinet only took the responsibility for the Minister's action if the Minister reported the matter to the Cabinet and obtained Cabinet's sanction before he put into effect this policy. Then the policy become the Cabinet policy and not only the Minister but the whole Cabinet ought to take the responsibility for whatever might have been done by a subordinate. In this case, therefore, Patel, who admittedly was acting as the Principal Secretary of the Minsitry, could not be fastened with the responsibility of having effected this transaction in his own secretarial capacity. The documents placed before the Commission established that the decision to buy further shares was approved by H.M. Patel on 24 June 1957. Whether the Minister was aware of what Patel had done or not, the fact was that when the latter came to know of the transaction, he never repudiated the action of Patel. Therefore, there was clear acquiescence on the part of the Minister in the role of Patel in bringing about the transaction of 24 June 1957. The lack of repudiation would go to support Patel's story that the Minister had approved the transaction in Bombay on 24 June 1957. The Minister had to fully and squarely accept the responsibility for what Patel did. If the transaction was improper and unjustified, although Patel might be actually responsible for the transaction, constitutionally the responsibility was that of the Minister.[4]

It was the lingering memory of the freedom movement and the high standards of rectitude in the matter of handling of public funds established by Mahatma Gandhi that helped preserve some norms of public conduct in the first years after independence. The political heir of the Mahatma Gandhi was then at the helm of affairs. A certain permissiveness, a certain laxity had begun to creep in. But Nehru loved Parliament and accepted wholeheartedly the principles of accountability of the Cabinet Ministers to Parliament in the matter of the actions of the Departments for which they were responsible. Inspite of his personal attachment to the Finance Minister T.T. Krishnamachari, he accepted the findings of the Chagla Commission and allowed TTK to go. He did not try to wriggle out by talking about the system failure or the complicated nature of the relationship between autonomous bodies, civil servants of the Government Departments and the limits of Ministerial responsibility. The Government Resolution of 27 May 1959 admitted that "the constitutional responsibility" of the Minister had been attracted and said that he had resigned as a consequence. Although Krishna Menon was very close to him, Nehru ultimately accepted his resignation on the issue of lack of Defence preparedness after the debacle of the border war with China in 1962. Nehru got the K.D. Malaviya matter inquired into by S.K. Das (J), who held him guilty. Nehru asked Malaviya to resign in 1963. Things began to change thereafter, and under Mrs. Gandhi, Rajiv Gandhi and their successors, it came to be established that the Ministers in the good books of the Prime Minister are never responsible for any scams or lapses, grave or otherwise.

An example should suffice, the one about C. Subramaniam, under Mrs. Gandhi. The change of attitude was quite sharp.

The 50th Report of the PAC in the Third Lok Sabha contained the findings of the Committee's investigation into the Steel Barter Deal. C. Subramaniam, the Minister then in charge of the Ministry of Steel and Heavy Industry, had, while speaking in Parliament, alleged that the PAC had drawn its conclusions without taking into consideration all the facts. The Minister was thereupon given an opportunity to give his evidence before the PAC although the request was "unusual" and had came late and had "caused some avoidable inconvenience to the Committee". C. Subramaniam met the PAC on 1 August 1966. The Committee was not convinced by the Minister's explanation. It held that the Minister's remarks on the PAC's conclusion were "rather unfortunate". The Minister, when confronted with the evidence placed before the Committee during his deposition, had no choice but to agree that the PAC "was fully justified in making the observation in para 4.128 of the 50th Report." The PAC castigated the Ministry for not framing its blacklisting order in clearer terms so that there would be no possibility of its being interpreted differently. The PAC was unable to understand why the Minister changed his previous order asking for suspension of business with the Amichand Pyarelal group of firms.

The Iron and Steel Controller did not implement the original order. He made two references to the Ministry seeking explanations. The Minister's orders had been leaked out, for the Controller's Office was in league with the firms, and there was lobbying for getting it changed. There was a representation from the firms to the Ministry and a meeting with the Minister took place on 20 July 1963. The reasons for the revision of the order were "somewhat obscure", the Committee said, adversely commenting on the then Steel Minister's conduct.[5] However, my attempts to secure his resignation failed. There was a difference between the approach of Nehru and his daughter. Moral considerations and points of propriety did not carry much weight with her. Mrs. Gandhi agreed to an inquiry, but told me not to press for his resignation. She made it clear to me that she would not accept it.

I need not enlarge here on the Bofors JPC Report. The Committee was boycotted by the main Opposition parties, not wisely, I think, and the Congress-dominated Committee did a complete whitewashing job. Its conclusions were that a correct procedure in gun selection was followed, the right gun was chosen, proper guarantees were offered, there was no bribe taken by officers or members of the Government, no extraneous influences were involved, there were no middlemen and the payments by Bofors such as winding up charges did not violate the Indian laws.

The subject matter of the latest JPC report involved fundamental questions about the functioning of the financial and banking systems, of the stock exchanges, in the liberal regime of market economy, the available mechanisms of regulation and control, the autonomy of the Reserve Bank, of the nationalised credit institutions, the interaction between these institutions and the Ministry, and, finally, the relationship between the top civil servants of the Ministry and the Cabinet Minister.

The Government of India had, it might be recalled, in a Resolution of 27 May 1959 spelt out its position in the area of autonomous Corporations and the Government Departments. The Reserve Bank was already functioning as an autonomous body; the life insurance companies had been nationalised and an autonomous Corporation—the Life Insurance Corporation—had been set up under a Charter approved by Parliament. Jawaharlal Nehru was then the Prime Minister and G.B. Pant, the Home Minister. The Government resolution said: "The Government of India fullv appreciate that it is essential that the authority and powers of such corporations should be clearly defined under the relevant statute or charter and normally the corporation should function freely within the field so defined. But, in the very terms of the charter, certain matters mainly, but not entirely, of policy, would be specifically reserved for the Government. The 'autonomous functioning' of a corporation would mean 'free functioning' of that body within the terms of the charter and in conformity with the policy and guidance of Government given from time to time. *The responsibility for supervising, guiding and directing the body in order to ensure its proper working rests on Government. They have to assume that responsibility to enable them to discharge their duty to Parliament.* It is the responsibility of Government to take appropriate remedial action if and when the working of a corporation so requires. Excessive formalisation of the relations between the Government and the corporation would be unworkable and undesirable. *It follows, therefore, that the legal provisions regarding the power to give directions to a corporation should not be so construed as to prevent Government from having recourse to other channels of communication, such as informal discussion or conferences. There is no reason why Government should confine their contact with a corporation merely to giving statutory directions.*"[6]

When this was the official stand of the Government about autonomous corporations—and umpteen instances of interference and interventions by the Ministries in the working of these bodies can be cited in the subsequent period—how could the Ministers claim that they were not accountable for their grave failures? The JPC puts the matter very cogently. The indictment is unanswerable.

The key passage underlines the total lack of accountability at all levels of the Government: "The scam is basically a deliberate and criminal misuse of Public funds through various types of securities transactions with the aim of illegally siphoning of funds of banks and PSUs to select brokers for speculative returns. The latest irregularities in the securities and banking transactions, are manifestations of this chronic disorder since they involved not only the Banks but also the stock market, financial institutions, PSU, the central bank of the country and even the Ministry of Finance, and other economic Ministries in varying degrees. The most unfortunate aspect has been the emergence of a culture of non-accountability which permeated all sections of the Government and Banking system over the years. The state of the country's system of governance, the persistence of non-adherence to rules, regulations and guidelines, the alarming decay over time in the banking systems has been fully exposed.... Through all these years the ability of the concerned authorities to effectively address themselves to the problems has been tested and found wanting."[7]

Dr. Manmohan Singh, Finance Minister, told the JPC: "As regards the functions of the FM, he oversees the work of the Ministry and provides overall policy guidance to the officials. Revenue and Expenditure decisions are the direct responsibility of the Finance Ministry. As such FM has more direct responsibility in these areas. He is also responsible for broad policy decisions affecting the financial system where the Finance Ministry is involved. However, FM cannot be held responsible for administrative failures or management deficiencies in the case of individual banks and other financial institutions."[8]

The statement of Dr. Manmohan Singh was brazen, to say the least. It negated the position which is universally accepted in Britain and in India. The instances given and the policy elucidated in the Government Resolution under Nehru of 27 May 1959 cited above correctly sets out the true position. The Committee was justified in rejecting the FM's contention and in saying that distinction made by Dr. Singh could not be sustained by the parliamentary government's theory and practice.

The question I wish to raise here is the role of the Opposition in the JPC affair. The Report was a unanimous Report. The Congress Party had a majority on the Committee. *There was absolutely no need to discuss the Report. All that the Opposition should have demanded was expeditious action on the recommendations of the Committee.* Obviously this could not have been done within a week.

Why then did the Opposition force a debate? By insisting on this and linking it up with resignation of Dr. Manmohan Singh—and two others—*it got the Report virtually rejected by Parliament.* The Ministerial aspirants on the Congress Benches went on a rampage, so to say, and ridiculed the Report, the Committee Members and the Chairman, R.N. Mirdha. A.B. Vajpayee is a veteran parliamentarian. *It is amazing that Vajpayee wanted a discussion and that too under Rule 184 and a vote at the end of it!* Indrajit Gupta also has three or four decades' parliamentary experience. Somanath Chatterjee is not a new comer. Similarly, the Janata Dal, too, has experienced members. It would have been best if the Report had been left alone as suggested by Kamal Morarka in the Rajya Sabha. The Opposition wanted a discussion and ruling party set a trap by quickly conceding it and seized the opportunity to denigrate the Report. There were hundred ways of prodding the Government into implementation of the Report. But the Opposition did not want that. Ram Nivas Mirdha, chairman of the JPC, expressed his displeasure over the discussion of the committee's unanimous report in the Lok Sabha. The general practice, he rightly said, was not to have a debate on these reports, certainly not before the government had an opportunity to consider the report and its recommendations. After examining such reports, the government first submits its action-taken-report. The JPC may, if it thinks necessary, react to the action-taken-report. It is only at that stage that a discussion can be raised on the areas of disagreement between the government and the JPC. Instead of following this time-honoured procedure a debate was held in the Lok Sabha whose outcome can only be described as unfortunate. It had the intended or unintended effect of debunking the unanimous report.

The Opposition's condition is truly pathetic. There cannot be any coordination between the non-Congress Parties in the existing circumstances. By adopting an extremist course the BJP has antagonised all other non-Congress Opposition parties. The BJP had strongly backed liberalisation. L.K. Advani spoke as the Government's Economic-Ambassador-at-large when he went abroad two years ago. The Jaswant Singhs and Pramod Mahajans are the strongest adherents of the market economy and all that it means. I have carefully gone through the report. It has not accused any minister of taking bribes. As Mirdha said, many charges had been made against ministers outside, but no evidence was produced against any individual minister. The ministers have not been accused of any moral turpitude. Their responsibility relates to administrative failure. They tolerated continued unaccountability at all levels and a criminal violation of guidelines. They must assume "constructive responsibility" for these lapses. But no minister was prepared to accept this constitutional responsibility honestly and frankly.

The Finance Ministry only talked of the system failure. Chidambaram spoke of collective responsibility of the Ministry to Parliament and of individual Ministers to the Prime Minister. The learned constitutional expert has probably not heard of the individual Cabinet member's responsibility for what happens in his Department. He probably has not heard of individual Minister's being censured by Parliament in Britain. He does not obviously know that we in India also have introduced Censure Motions in our Lok Sabha to haul up individual Cabinet Ministers.

The CPI-M spokesman lavished praise on Dr. Manmohan Singh's personal integrity. That was irrelevant. Indrajit Gupta wanted him to rest on a high moral pedestal. But what if he does not like to stay there?

Indrajit Gupta talked of a particular mindset and explained the failure in terms of the mindset. He thought that the Finance Minister was a "prisoner of this mindset" and believed "blindly in the infallibility of the market system". That probably accounted for the plunder and boom of 1992. The Swatantrites, I remember, used to explain past failures in terms of a different mindset: belief in the central command system, efficacy of centralised planning, the virtues of the expanding public sector and so on. I am suspicous of this mindset theory. It destroys all personal responsibility. Everybody by now knows that Stalin and his henchmen liquidated over 20 million innocent people. Some put the figure much higher. If you talk of systemic failure or attribute all crimes to a particularly rigid mindset, then nobody was responsible for the above cold-blooded liquidation, neither Stalin nor his henchmen.

So there was this strange consensus on the system failure, on the mind-

sets which actually caused the Scam. There was no human failure, they all seemed to contend. No, the systems are not operated by human beings. They just run, and sometimes develop faults. No human being is really responsible. Definitely not the Cabinet Ministers, nor the Governor of the Reserve Bank nor Secretaries of the Government Departments from Under-Secretary up. The Chairmen of the nationalised credit institutions were, of course, not responsible. Nor for that matter the chiefs of the Foreign Banks, who it was said, treated the Reserve Bank and other regulatory mechanisms with contempt, can be blamed.

If there was a human failure at all it was, *perhaps*, at the level of Section Officers or Upper Division Clerks, or, *more probably*, at the level of computer boys and girls, who were not able to decipher the data on the floppies, or Lower Division Clerks; anyway the failure, *most certainly*, was at the level of peons who carried files from cabin to cabin or one office to another. Suspend a few of them, don't touch the great indispensables like Dr. Manmohan Singh, Shankaranand or Rameshwar Thakur and everything would be fine. The system would then correct itself and the mindset, too, would change for the better!

References

1. R.N. Mirdha, *JPC Report on Stock Market Scam*, 1993, p. 3.
2. *Committee on the Conduct of a Member* (The Mudgal Case), New Delhi, 1951, pp. 1-29.
3. Herbert Morrison, *Government and Parliament—A Survey from the Inside*, London, 1954, pp. 323-24.
4. *Report of the M.C. Chagla Commission of Inquiry into the Affairs of the LIC of India, 1958*, p. 23.
5. *50th and 55th Reports of the PAC*, Third Lok Sabha, New Delhi, 1966, pp. 92 and v, 10, 12 and 13 respectively.
6. *Report of the Vivian Bose Board of Inquiry*, pp. 1-5.
7. *JPC Report*, p. 7.
8. *Ibid*, p. 223.

15

LEGISLATURES' OVERSENSITIVENESS ON THE QUESTION OF THEIR PRIVILEGES

I have been a votary of parliamentary democracy. No form of government is ideal. But in Indian conditions, I think, the federal parliamentary democracy is the most suitable form of government. Any presidential system, whether patterned after the United States or France, would soon prove to be unworkable and create a constitutional impasse.

In a parliamentary system the members of the political executive, that is the Cabinet, are recruited from within the Legislature. If an outsider is recruited as a Minister, he has to get himself elected to Parliament. If he fails to do that, on the expiration of the six-month period, he automatically ceases to be a Minister. To reappoint him again as a Minister within a day or two would be a blatant violation of the Constitution. In the United States the "Cabinet" can be recruited from outside; in fact if a Congressman or Senator is appointed to the "Cabinet", he has to resign from the Legislature. The Legislatures do not want to have Presidential agents in their midst. They jealously guard their independence and privileges. The Houses of Legislatures enjoy certain privileges to prevent obstruction and impeding of the performance by them of their functions, and to punish offences against their dignity and authority. The power to punish contempt has, historically descended from the *lex et consuetudo parliamenti. Like all powers this power too might be and is, not unoften, misused. And so this calls for caution and restraint.*

Our Constitution provides that the Council of Ministers shall be responsible to the directly-elected House of the People—the Lok Sabha. In theory the Prime Minister and Council are the creatures of Parliament. But in fact the dominance of Parliament is a fiction *most of the time.* I say most of the time on purpose. For as long as the Prime Minister has the confidence of the Party of which he is the head and which has a majority in the House, the constitutional supremacy of the Lok Sabha has no practical significance. The modern parties are well-disciplined parties, and the Congress party is our country's first modern party. Its internal discipline was quite loose in the first fifty years. True the Swarajya Party—which was essentially a parliamentary party—was known for its tight discipline. But it was always in the opposition and its discipline was never put to the test. With the inaugration of Provincial Autonomy in 1937, the Congress Legislature Parties underwent a transformation, and the British rulers soon discovered that its Ministers could not be manipulated as the non-Congress Ministers under Dyarchy—Montagu-Chelmsford Reforms—could be manipulated by the powerful Governors. In the post-freedom era, the Congress Party's discipline has been exemplary.

The British Conservative Party has a long tradition of dissent. The Tory members freely exercise conscience vote, but are never penalised on that account. The Labour Party is comparatively less tolerant, but the Labour members enjoy great latitude and record, not rarely, dissenting votes. The Congress Party at the Centre has a complete hold over its members. In the first, second, third, sixth and seventh Lok Sabhas it had more than two-thirds majority. In the fourth Lok Sabha it did not command such a huge majority, but compared to British majorities of the last four decades, its majority was quite comfortable till, of course, the notorious Congress split of 1969 reduced it to a minority. In the present Lok Sabha it was in a minority; at the time of every discussion on President's address or the Budget or the no-confidence motions, newspapers filled their columns predicting the fall of the P.V.R. Government or at least its finding itself in dire straights. But the sequel was always a farce and an anti-climax. Only the newspapers lost credibility.

The Congress being, thus, the leading party in the country, it ought to give a lead to all the majorities in the various Legislatures in the matter of conducting its daily proceedings in a meaningful manner, and, more importantly, *in exercising the awesome powers the Constitution has conferred on the Legislatures under Articles 105 (Union) and 194 (States) in a restrained manner.* In my day, I used the weapon of breach of privilege and contempt of the Lok Sabha quite frequently and in an effective manner. The huge tome of the *Privilege Digest* tells at least a part of the story. But I rarely used that weapon against exercise of freedom of expression by the press or writers. While I always urge self-restraint on the part of the Executive, the Legislature and the Judiciary, I must address the same prayer to the press, for it also is a pillar of democracy. It was called the Fourth Estate. I feel sad that many members of the new generation of journalists neither value accuracy in the matter of facts—I am not talking of their political views—nor seem to care much for restrained expression. Especially, in speaking of the higher judiciary and the Legislatures a certain deference is, I think, not out of place. I myself have harshly criticised the Legislatures and the Judiciary. But can we all the time attribute base, unworthy and ulterior motives and impeach their private character? *My privilege notices were mostly directed towards enforcing accountability of the Government to Parliament and the public.*

Most of the time the Ministers and their bureaucratic assistants are engaged in stonewalling questions and indulge in evasions, prevarication and even outright lies. Sometimes bureaucrats give false evidence before parliamentary committees. Sometimes members also engage in misconduct, they take bribes—the Mudgal case is well known. We used the privilege rules to haul up Ministers who told lies, not to harass critical journalists. Who does not know that many of the legislators sub-let their rooms and quarters at high "rents", trade the gas connections which they can now distribute, extract premium on the telephone allotments from the quotas given to them under the new-fangled schemes. *Of course, there are some honourable exceptions!* Now why should not vigilant and public-spirited legislators, journalists and members of the public attack these malpractices? I had hauled up an officer who gave false evidence on oath in the notorious Steel Barter Case of the sixties, and he was called to the bar of the House and reprimanded. I arraigned Mrs. Indira Gandhi herself for harassing four officers for daring to collect information for parliamentary questions on Maruti. But in the Indira Case, despite my appeal for self-restraint, the JPP's angry majority led by the Ram Jelthmalanis, Subramaniam Swamys, George Fernandess—and how sad! Morarji Desais—sent Mrs. Gandhi to jail. It created a sympathy wave for her. The punishment given was wrong. A simple admonition would have served the purpose.

These days it is not so much Parliament but the State Legislatures who are flexing their muscles and making an exhibition of their ugly intolerance. The Tamilnadu and Maharashtra Assemblies have abandoned self-limitation and self-control and are issuing warrants against journalists and editors and threatening to punish them and have, in some cases, already done so. The Madras High Court has intervened in one case, but in Maharashtra the Assembly proceeded to send Nikhil Wagle of *Mahanagar* to jail for four days. How its honour was enhanced by this show of churlishness, I fail to understand. It is significant that a mature politician like Sharad Pawar, instead of using his immense prestige to restrain the angry members, himself sponsored the deplorable resolution. *Everybody knows about his clandestine relations with all manner of Mafiasi and so, although he has the hide of a hippopotamus, he is all the time afraid of exposure.* It is a pity that like Sharad Pawar, Ms. Jayalalitha, though popular, is also becoming intolerant. Both Pawar and Ms. Jayalalitha should remember that they both are human beings and not a God and a Goddess respectively. The Speakers, too, are failing in their duty to curb these outbursts of hysteria; they ought, I think, to put their foot down.

If the Legislatures run amuck—as the House of Commons had done in the 19th century, committing all and sundry to the Tower of London—and start sending people to jail, they will loose the respect of the electorate. Let them remember that their membership of the Assembly has a fixed term. Their job is not permanent. It can be terminated by the people.

After the November 1993 Assembly elections some newspapers published reports to the effect that over 700 history sheeters, that is persons with criminal record had offered themselves as candidates in U.P. Most were rejected by the voters but 106 were successful. Among those successful candidates, the BJP led with 44 MLAs, closely followed by the Samajvadi Dal, and also the BSP, the

Congress, the Janata Dal and the CPI. Now is the U.P. Legislature going to start contempt proceedings against M.A. Hafiz of the *Hindustan Times* and me for publicising this unsavoury fact? It is time the political parties, the Legislatures, *and the Judiciary*, the bureaucracy and police at all levels and also the Fourth Estate reformed themselves. Otherwise they will face, before long, civil disobedience, by a swelling army of dissenters, who will refuse in true Gandhian spirit to indulge in breast beating, but silently suffer in a good and righteous cause. It will be the Legislatures, I warn, which will, ultimately, forfeit the nation's confidence.

16

A WELTER OF JUDICIAL DECISIONS

The decisions of our highest judicial tribunal are increasingly becoming a riddle. The plethora of opinions being delivered—most of them not dissenting judgements but concurring opinions—are a source of confusion. To agree with the colleague delivering the main opinion is apparently considered *infra dig* by others even though they do not basically differ from the opinion. In these days of the sky rocketting prices of paper, the verbosity of judicial opinions in nothing less than frightening. It is not always clear what the decision and *ratio decidendi* is and what is in the nature of *obiter dicta*. The judges make pronouncements on matters which are not before the Court for decision, matters which have not been carefully and fully argued by the opposing counsel. The judges also feel themselves free to disregard the clear words of the Constitution and substitute for these words expressions of their own choice. If the Constitution says that certain appointments should be made "in consultation with" some authority, the judges would change "consultation" into "concurrence". The power of veto would be read into the word consultation. Where a general expression "judges" in the plural, without a qualifying adjective, is used, the primacy of the Chief Justice is inferred by an abstruse process of interpretation.

The generally accepted pre-condition of adversary proceedings is being increasingly ignored. Abstract questions are taken up for judicial pronouncements, instead of the judges willingly and strictly functioning and deciding within the framework of concrete issues and cases.

Our Constitution is based on the concept of limited powers. It is the Constitution and the people who are supreme. But we often forget this. From the days of the Nath Pai Bill "the principle of the sovereignty of Parliament" held the field. The so-called high principle and the whole philosophy behind it produced the frightful 19 months of the Emergency raj. Now the pendulum has swung to the other extreme, and we are about to enthrone the theory of judicial sovereignty. Instead of exercising the power of judicial review with an amount of caution and self-restraint, we see its scope being extended everyday.

Often Supreme Court judges hand down contradictory opinions, because the judges either do not know what other benches have decided, or because they think it wiser to turn a blind eye to these decisions.

I find it difficult to reconcile the opinions delivered and observations made by the judges of the same Court on the powers of the Chief Election Commission and on the mode of decision-making in the multi-member Commission whose responsibility it is to conduct the election. These baffling pronouncements are unintentionally encouraging the Chief Election Commission's reckless adventures.

Here I wish to examine the latest decision of the Supreme Court on the ambit of Presidential power under Article 356.

First of all let me state that a special bench of seven judges had meticulously gone into the question of the scope of judicial review under this article. There was absolutely no need to constitute a larger bench to examine the matter afresh. All the three cases of Karnataka, Meghalaya and MP-HP-Rajasthan could have been satisfactorily decided on the basis of the Rajasthan Case. But under the pressure of counsel—who have a vested interest in endless litigation—a larger bench was created.

The Presidential Proclamation in Nagaland on 7 August 1988 was held to be invalid on the ground that Vamuzo was not given an opportunity to form a Ministry and prove his majority on the floor of the Assembly. The Maghalaya action under Article 356 on 11 October 1989 was held to be unconstitutional because the material on which it was based was *prima facie* "irrational" and vitiated by "factual and legal *malafide.*" The Karnataka Proclamation of 24 April 1989 was faulted on the ground that the "facts" stated by the Governor were really not facts but his own subjective opinion based on unascertained facts and not on any objective material on which the President could have acted. However, since in these States new Assemblies had started functioning long back (in fact, a new poll is due in Karnataka this year), the findings had no practical effect.

While the Karnataka High Court judgement was subjected to close scrutiny by the Court, the judgement of the Madhya Pradesh High Court was not critically examined at all. A discussion of the MP decision would, I think, have thrown light on some aspects of the Case. But the decision of the said High Court was sidetracked by taking the high road of secularism. I remember that the then CJ Bhagvati had also decided the Case of the Repromulgation of Ordinances without reference to the decision of the Allahabad High Court, which, in my view, was better articulated than the Bhagvati judgement. However, the former CJ of the Supreme Court did not have the courtesy to mention the Allahabad High Court's decision, leave alone expressing his concurrence with it.

Possibly piqued by the impossibility of granting relief in the Karnataka, Meghalaya and Nagaland Cases—in my opinion these Cases should not have been taken up at all since elections had already been held there—the Supreme Court majority decided on *a priori* basis that the Court had the power to revive dead Assemblies. It also held that the President cannot dissolve the Assembly before the parliamentary approval of the Proclamation under 356. It further claimed that the Supreme Court had the power to issue an injunction to prevent holding of a fresh election and thereby pre-empt the voters' right to elect a new Assembly.

The MP-HP-Rajasthan Case was decided on the basis of the principle that the secular order is a basic feature of the Constitution. I would have personally liked the issue to have been settled on the basis of the violation of the constitutional order. After all what the UP Government had done—and the other three State Governments had abetted the UP Government—was to destroy the Rule of Law and deliberately flout the affidavits freely made before the Supreme Court. Sunderlal Patwa had accepted responsibility for the demolition of the Mosque and had sought the electorate's verdict on the Sangh Pariwar's "6 December Action Plan."

But anyway this is a small matter. What distressed me was that portion of the majority judgements which pronounced on an issue which was really not for decision before the great tribunal. In Karnataka and Meghalaya new Assemblies were elected and were functioning. *No authority under the Constitution has been given the power to replace a newly elected Assembly by an old Assembly which had been dissolved.* Nor has the Constitution clothed any authority with the power to interfere with the electoral process set in motion after the dissolution of the old Assembly. The period of President's rule initially is only two months and this can be extended upto *a period of not more than one year* with the approval of the two Houses of Parliament [Clause (5), Article 356].

The latest decision of the Supreme Court claims the power to bring to life a dissolved Assembly and direct the Government not to hold fresh elections. Assuming the Court finds that the imposition of President's rule and dissolution of the Assembly on account of irrelevant and extraneous reasons was unconstitutional, it could direct holding of *immediate* elections—instead of holding them anytime within one year. But the majority of the nine-judge bench reads into the Constitution a limitation on the President's power to dissolve the State Assembly, although the Constitution in terms says that President may assume to himself "all or any of the powers vested in or exercisable by the Governor". [Article (1) (a) 356]. The Governor's powers include the power to dissolve the Assembly. It is true this power, in a Cabinet form of Government, has to be exercised on the advice of a popular Ministry. But under President's rule the advice would be not of the State Ministry which has been disbanded but the Central Cabinet.

The power to dissolve the Assembly has nothing to do with the approval of the Proclamation by the two Houses of Parliament. If dissolution is to be made conditional on Parliament's approval, it would mean substituting for the Central Cabinet's advice the Central Legislature's advice for this purpose. Is the Supreme Court free to rewrite the Constitution as it likes?

In fact I would have appreciated if the Supreme Court had decided that under President's rule there should be no "animated suspension" of the Assembly which is used to inspire defections as in Gujarat in 1976 or to resolve the Congress Party's internal factional conflicts (as in Andhra Pradesh during the Telangana agitation in the early seventies). To deny the President the right to dissolve the Assembly or to claim the right to revive a dead Assembly is rank interference at the expense of a coordinate branch of the Government. But to preach self-restraint and caution is, perhaps, an anarchronism in this age of Self-aggrandisement, Consumerism and Permissiveness.

Curiously, the Special Bench majority has not even thought out the implications of its decision. It is known that in the 1977 Rajasthan Case it was unanimously held by a seven-judge bench that on the basis of the material and reasoning disclosed in Home Minister Charan Singh's letter, the imposition of President's rule in the eight States where the Congress had been totally routed would be justified. Now let us apply the decision of the latest majority (consisting of Sawant, R. Pandian, Jeevan Reddy and S.C. Agrawal (JJ) to this situation created after Indira Gandhi's defeat in 1977. What would have happened? *The said Assemblies could not have been dissolved before the approval of the Proclamation by the two Houses of the Union Legislature.* The Lok Sabha would have approved it by a comfortable majority. But in the Rajya Sabha the Congress was strongly entrenched and the approval motion would have been defeated by a convincing majority. Since each House has to approve the Presidential action a complete deadlock would have been reached. Any pronouncement by the Supreme Court on the validity of the Proclamation would in this situation have become irrelevant. *For Parliamentary approval has nothing to do with constitutionality. The decision of the two Houses would be political. Similarly, the ultimate popular verdict also has nothing to do with the constitutional validity or the invalidity of the Presidential Proclamation.* The Karnataka electorate punished the Janata Party for wrongfully removing the Devraj Urs Ministry. But the voters in the same State, in the 1989 election, did not show much sympathy for S.R. Bommai's badly divided Party, the dismissal of whose Government the Supreme Court has now held invalid. Similarly, Tamilnadu electorate in 1991 did not punish the Congress-Jayalalitha combination which had secured Karunanidhi's ouster under Article 356. The voter is influenced by non-legal considerations. The intervention of the Courts, one would think, in this political conflict, is totally inappropriate. But where angels would fear to tread, our judges are willing to walk in eagerly. Unfortunately, just as authoritarian Indira Gandhi, supported by a section of the Left, was fired by the idea of parliamentary supremacy and sovereignty in the sixties and early seventies, so in the post-Emergency period the judges and the bar—for self-serving purposes—seem to have been inflamed by the doctrine of the absolute supremacy of the Courts. Parliament supremacywallas turned dictator (Indira Gandhi) can be and indeed were corrected by the electorate (as in 1977), but who will correct our judges?

The Court first reads into Article 356 its right to revive a dead Assembly and since it cannot be squared with the scheme of that Article, it cites the dubious example of Pakistan and directs that no Assembly can be dissolved before the approval of the Presidential Proclamation by Parliament. (In Pakistan the Army Chief of Staff kicked out the President, the Prime Minister, the Speaker and Chief Minister and intimidated the Supreme Court into deafening silence). The majority of our Court, nevertheless, has said that the Court can even postpone the holding of elections in order to enable it to decide the constitutionality of the action under Article 356. This goes against the absolute right of the people to elect a government of their choice. If any wrong has been done by the Centre it can be set right by the people. I fear that the decision of the nine-judge bench—four judges have strongly dissented—is bound to create problems. Ignoring the 1977 precedent, making abstract pronouncements and arguing back from on *a priori* determination, made without reference to, in fact, in opposition to the constitutional provisions—namely the assertion of the power to revive a dead Assembly—is fraught, I fear, with the most harmful consequences.

There are some unsavoury aspects of our judicial proceedings, of which senior lawyers are an important part, which I cannot help mentioning. The lawyers, perhaps, have their own convenient and self-serving Code of Conduct. How can they refuse to "serve" their clients when they approach them? But to me it is absolutely disgusting that people as politicians and former Law Ministers should support and sponsor legislation incorporating one opinion and argue against the same legislation and opinion in the higher courts in their capacity as counsel for a fat fee. This is nothing short of dishonesty, a practice which Mahatma Gandhi as a lawyer found so distasteful. This double-faced policy of some senior advocates adds to the confusion of judicial decision making.

One final observation. The attitude of some of my Socialist friends quite intrigues me. They denounced the Presidential Proclamation in the BJP States. But they were very much a party as Ministers to the decision to dissolve the Assemblies without obtaining parliamentary approval in 1977: They even supported the totally unjustified dismissal of the Devraj Urs Ministry in 1978. And yet they hail the new majority opinion as a landmark judgement. It is a topsy-turvy world.

17

WILL EXPANDED STATE AUTONOMY HELP?

The events of 6 December 1992 and after have without doubt shaken the Constitutional scheme to its foundation and have put a question mark on the championship of the principle of extended State Autonomy by Leftist parties and regional political groups. In the twenties and thirties the Muslim League was the most ardent advocate of the principle of Provincial Autonomy. The Act of 1935, while preserving the supremacy of the Central Government, had granted considerable powers to the Provincial Governments. The Congress, although an advocate of a strong Centre, agreed through its 8 August 1942 resolution to a federal constitution with the largest measure of autonomy for the Provinces. It also conceded that the residuary powers would be with constituent units and not the federal union. This did not, however, satisfy the Muslim League. By now it was committed to partition. Jinnah, who was at heart a centraliser and, in his phase as a doughty champion of united India, had, with Tej Bahadur Sapru, demanded a strong Centre to curb India's innate fissiparous tendencies, would be satisfied with nothing but separation. He intended to set up a centralised state in the Muslim-majority areas and bury Provincial Autonomy. The events of 1946-47 shattered the dreams of the Congress leaders. After the terrible Calcutta killings of August 1946 and the tragic happenings in Noakhali and Tipperah, the Congress repeatedly asked the Viceroy to apply Section 93 (similar to the present Article 356) to Bengal. We cannot go into Section 93. We cannot do this under the scheme of Provincial Autonomy, Wavell maintained.

The traumatic experience induced the Congress leadership to modify the contemplated federal scheme and go in for "a Union of States". The Constitution as it emerged from the Constituent Assembly not only differed from the semi-confederal framework expounded in the 16 May 1946 Cabinet Mission Plan, but it even differed from the 8 August 1942 resolution. It placed the superior authority in the hands of the Union, conferred residuary powers on the Centre and put the States in a position of subordination to the Union. The Supreme Court might have described the federal structure as a basic feature of our Constitution, but a close perusal of the various provisions of Part XI on Relations between the Union and the States, and Articles 355, 356, 357, 365 and so on can leave no doubt that it is the Union Centre which has been given the decisive voice.

The abuse of Article 356 by the Congress—and then also by other parties—created a widespread aversion from an over-centralised polity. *But life is very complex and historical development does not conform to any pre-determined pattern or abstract principles.* The situation, which faced the Centre in an acute form in December 1992 was absolutely extraordinary. It makes one sit up and take notice of the new challenges which our constitutional order faces. The problem of insurgency and terrorism in the North-west and North-east, though extremely serious, was of a different order, *although it involved a prolonged breakdown of constitutional government and necessitated recourse to Central rule whether exercised in the name of the President or the Governor even beyond the maximum period of three years laid down in Article 356(4).* In order to deal with the conditions in Punjab the Constitution had to be amended *three* times through the 64th, 68th and 69th Constitution (Amendment) Acts. In the State of J and K the constitutional provisions have been stretched and the requisite consent of the State Government has been interpreted not as the consent of an elected government but as the State Administration under the Governor. The UP crisis of 1992 was a different conundrum altogether. Here was a Party which claims to operate within the constitutional system. It has grown into a large Party. In both the Houses its leaders are the official leaders of the Opposition, enjoying Cabinet status, drawing emoluments and enjoying perks under a statute passed by Parliament. The Party was running not one, but four State Governments. Now what happens if such an outfit succeeds in rousing public hysteria, and enlists the support of a hundred thousand volunteers or more with the help of its State Governments and starts the operation of demolishing religious shrines belonging to the Muslim minority on the ground that these were, originally, Hindu temples and that this destruction was the necessary process of undoing "historical wrongs"? Had the Party proclaiming this programme been a small party it could have been easily curbed with the minimum application of force. *But what is to happen in a case where a big party which after the dismissal of its State Governments and a spell of President's rule has been returned to power—for the elections are unavoidable—and then repeat in Mathura and Kashi what happened at Ayodhya?* What is the Centre to do in that eventuality? It is necessary to seriously ponder over this dire possibility, however, remote it might be. True,Centre is not entirely helpless, constitutionally speaking. There is, for instance, Article 256 which gives the Union power to issue directions to a State for the purpose of enforcing compliance with the laws applicable in that State. This provision could have been used even in December 1992. The Centre could have issued a formal direction to the Government that it obey the Court orders and strictly apply the laws. But how is the Centre ensure that the direction is obeyed? What if the State quite deliberately disobeyed the instructions? Again resort to Article 356? Imagine the terrible consequences of the repetition of this process? It's effect on the *morale* of the services and the police? *At the end of it all the administration would become totally non-functional. Chaos would ensue.* Perhaps, it might be said that instead of having recourse to this extreme measure, the Centre might deploy its forces and itself protect the places of worship, and, in the case of serious riots, send its para-military forces or army to quell the disturbances. But under the existing constitutional provisions this cannot be done without the consent of the States. It might be remembered that Kalyan Singh had objected to the Centre's increasing the strength of the Central forces and had stopped them from entering the environs of the Babri Masjid-Ramjanmabhoomi structure. Mrs. Indira Gandhi had introduced a new Article 257-A through the 42nd Constitutional Amendment Act. The new Article said that the Union could deploy its forces to meet grave threats to law and order and require the States to follow its direction in regard to their deployment.

The non-Congress Opposition (including myself) had then opposed this new Article and the 44th Amendment had omitted it.

Article 257-A might have come in handy in the situation created in UP in (July and) December 1992 and might have been useful in future also. *But again the abstraction of State Autonomy and fear of its abuse would not permit its restoration.*

The proposal which the Centre is reportedly contemplating about a Constitutional amendment and prohibition of communal and religious propaganda and organization will be a non-starter. P.V. Narasimha Rao is scarcely serious about fighting communalism. He is flirting with his own brand of *sadhus* and *yajnas*. The result was the disaster of *soma yajna* at Ayodhya. For their own reasons Arjun Singh, Sharad Pawar and Karunakaran are opposed to a ban on communal parties. Most people in Bhopal know that Arjun Singh and Sunder Lal Patwa have been chums; Sharad and Shiv Sena's Balasaheb Thakre are secret allies and Karunakaran and the Muslim League in Kerala are open partners. These leaders say that the communal parties be fought politically. Who will fight them? The JD has broken into pieces, and the Congress is deeply mired in factional warfare. Neither the Rajasthan, MP and UP Congress bosses nor JD faction leaders in UP can moderate their personal egos. That the BJP also is developing factionalism is poor consolation.

The power maniacs and incarnations of Gods in the Janata fragments and the feuding Congress politicians are unwillingly working for the return of the BJP to power whose tide has begun to recede. People have had enough of demolitions, riots and bomb blasts. Will the chanting of *mantras* like State Autonomy or the grandiose statements of the Left Parties about massive popular campaigns—which never take off in the vast Hindi belt and Western India—be of any help at all? The resurgence of the forces of social justice and equality, and, above all, the good sense of our voters is our only hope. The campaigns of Mulayam Singh in UP and the Madhavrao Scindia initiative in Madhya Pradesh provide a silver lining in an otherwise dreary political outlook. At the same time the statements of V.P. Singh, Rambilas Paswan, Omprakash Chautala and Ajit Singh do not give any ground for hope about the Janata Dal's recovery in the key State of UP. The shortsighted policy which has led to a conflict between the CPI and JD in Patna in the recent parliamentary election and the division of progressive vote is a harbinger of disaster. But who cares?

18

SHESHAN'S WAR ON CARPET-BAGGERS

It was the Union Constitution Committee which formulated the basic proposals for the setting up for a bicameral Legislature for the Union India. The main feature of these proposals were: that the two chambers should be named the Council of States and the House of the People, these names indicating the manner in which each chamber would be constituted; the House of the People would be directly elected by adult franchise from territorial constituencies; the Council of States would have 250 members; the State Assemblies would constitute its electoral college; the Vice-President of India would be *ex-officio* member of the Council of States and its Chairman; the two chambers would, except in respect of Money Bills, have equal powers and deadlocks would be resolved by joint meetings; Money Bills would originate in the House of the People and the power of the other House would be limited to making suggestions for amendment, which the House of the People could accept or reject; the Council of States would not be liable to dissolution, one-third of its members retiring every two years.

As will be noticed, when the Constitution came to be finally adopted no substantial changes were made in these proposals, except providing for nomination of twelve members who have special knowledge or practical experience in respect of such matters as literature, science, art and social services. The other seats in the Rajya Sabha were to be filled by election by the State Legislatures.

The opinion in the Constituent Assembly was sharply divided

on the question of having a Second Chamber. Some members felt that it would only be a clog in the wheel of progress. One critic thought it would only deflect the legislative machinery, obstruct or delay legislation for which the people have given their votes and involve considerable outlay. The Upper House would only aid the party bosses, he said, to distribute more patronage. *But this vocal critic conceded that while there was absolutely no need for a Second chamber in the constituent units of the Union, at the Union Centre it would be proper to provide for a Second Chamber to represent the interests of the constituent States.* (The supporters of Second Chamber later dismissed the argument of delay and said that despite there being only a Single Chamber at the Centre after the transfer of power in 1947 the passage of the Hindu Code Bill was delayed. The Bill was ultimately dropped and could be passed in instalments only in the First Lok Sabha elected under the new Constitution). Some members defended the creation of the Upper House as a necessary corrective to hasty legislation. It would be useful, as a House of revision and correction. Only the Second Chamber could give careful and leisurely thought to the various legislative proposals that might emanate from the body directly elected on the basis of adult franchise. Some others suggested that the existence of the Second Chamber would enable the various types of minorities to secure due representation in the Legislature. Ultimately a compromise was worked out. The States were given the right to dispense with the Second Chambers with the consent of Parliament. *The Upper House was however retained at the Centre chiefly to represent the functional interests of the provinces or States as they come to be called.*

The question is has the Rajya Sabha fulfilled the expectations of the Founding Fathers in the four decades of its existence? Has it effectively served the interests of the States which elect the members of the Upper House? It has to be admitted that the Rajya Sabha has woefully failed to articulate effectively the special point of view of the States on issues that come up before the House or strongly defend its interests. The reasons are not far to seek. *The membership of the Rajya Sabha has become so much patronage at the disposal of the Party bosses to be distributed by them without reference to the interests of the States.* The fact that the members are elected through indirect election by members of the State Assemblies on the basis of a variant of proportional representation makes its easy for leaders of all parties to select men and women of their own choice without the slightest regard to the candidates' knowledge and competence to represent the States.

Had there been a system of direct election of the Rajya Sabha members such as exists in the case of the Federal Senators in America, the Party bosses would not have picked up "carpet-baggers" to be their standard bearers at these polls, but only senior and respected public figures who had wide acceptance in the State concerned. *It was the unfortunate introduction of the principle of indirect election that has turned Rajya Sabha into a House of Patronage.* This has placed enormous power in the hands of the bosses, and monied people and the lobbyists. The Party leaders have used their control over the Party machine to secure for themselves backdoor entry into Parliament. Defeat at a direct election or inability to win a popular election has never prevented bosses (or their protegees) like Atal Bihari Vajpayee, L.K. Advani, Sikandar Bakht, Rajgopal and Vishnu Kant Sastri (JS-BJP), Bhupesh Gupta, (CPI), or S.R. Bommai and Inder Gujral (JD) from securing an easy berth in the Rajya Sabha. The Ruling Party and other parties were able to get their defeated Lok Sabha or Assembly candidates or their favourites elected to the Rajya Sabha and also subsequently inducted into the Cabinets. The cases of Pranab Mukerjee (Gujarat) and Manmohan Singh (Assam), prove the point. Such "indispensable" persons can be brought in from any State which happened to be under their control or in which they had the required number of members of the Assembly to secure the success of their candidates at the Rajya Sabha poll.

All this was done in blatant violation of the Constitution and the Law. The Representation of People Act, 1950, had laid down the conditions for the registration of voters. The conditions of registration of voters are two in number. He must (a) be 18 years of age and (b) be ordinarily resident in the constituency where he seeks registration. *According to Section (19) (1) it is not enough to possess an address or own a dwelling house in the area.* It may be asked as what happens to those who on account of government service or military duty or responsibility associated with elected offices, or other public offices, are required to remain away from their ordinary places of residence for long stretches of time? Sub-section

3 and sub-section(4) of Section 19 of the Representation of People Act, 1950, makes an exception in the case of these persons. Their staying away from their ordinary places of residence would not affect their competence to be put on the voters' list in that constituency.

The President, in consultation, with the Election Commission, issues a notification under sub-section (4) of Section 19 of the Act, which lists the offices excepted by this Act. These public offices include: the President of India, the Vice-President of India, Governors of States, Cabinet Minister of the Union or of any State, the Deputy Chairman and Members of the Planning Commission, the Ministers of the Union or of any State, the Speaker of the House of the People or any State Legislative Assembly, the Chairman of any State, Legislative Council, Lieutenant Governors of Union territories, the Deputy Speaker of the House of the People or of any State Legislative Assembly, the Deputy Chairman of the Council of States or of any State Legislative Council; and Parliamentary Secretaries of the Union or of any State.

All candidates outside the categories mentioned above, who seek elections from States or Union Territories other than their own State or Territory, are guilty of violating the Constitution and the Law. The vested interest of politicians and the atmosphere of permissiveness tolerated and even encouraged by the powers-that-be have created a situation where a demand is made that not this permissiveness should be ended and the law strictly enforced, but that the law be changed to suit the convenience of the patronage givers, the patronage seekers, the money bags and the lobbyists.

I am, personally, in entire agreement with T.N. Sheshan. I have in the past criticised some of his tantrums. I have not liked some of his actions which led to interference by Courts as in the matter of Assembly bye-elections in West Bengal and the bye-election to the Legislative Council in Maharashtra. But I must place on record my appreciation of the fact that he conducted in November 1993 the fairest election after 1980. I also feel that the new Order which he has issued is wholly within the four corners of the law. While some of those included in the list of Rajya Sabha members published by him such as Bhuvanesh Chaturvedi may not be violators of the law, most of them are. They and their sponsors as voters are liable to be prosecuted under the Representation of People Act as well as the Indian Penal Code.

As a matter of fact a case was initiated by a resident of Lashkar Constituency in Madhya Pradesh against the BJP President, L.K. Advani. Advani had sought the intervention of the MP High Court to secure the quashing of the charge. Not only the High Court refused to quash the lower Court's order, but it also directed it to frame charges against Advani's sponsor under the IPC. Sheshan's new campaign for purifying the Rajya Sabha election process will evoke wide public response. The number of people involved in the violation of the law in relation to the Rajya Sabha elections is small and the law can be enforced very easily provided there is the will to do it. T.N. Sheshan has shown the necessary determination and can easily ensure that his latest order is enforced. As for prosecuting the past violations, it is up to local *pro bono publico* of the type we saw in Madhya Pradesh. The EC can help them. Sheshan wants to take up the difficult question of the inflated election expenditure. But without legislation he cannot do much. India is in a worse condition than Italy in every respect. In Italy the common people have risen against the all-pervading corruption and mafia rule. If T.N. Sheshan can shake up the corrupt political establishment he will be considered by all well wishers of the country to have rendered a yeoman's service to the cause of democracy.

19

ENDLESS ELECTIONS CAUSE ADMINISTRATIVE PARALYSIS

There was a time when one used to talk of an election year. Then we had synchronised Lok Sabha and Assembly elections. That seemed natural because both the Lok Sabha and the State Assemblies had five year terms. And so an election year materialised once in five years. 1952, 1957, 1962 and 1967 were election years. But things changed after the dissolution of the Lok Sabha in December 1970. This delinked the Lok Sabha and the Assembly elections. Whether this delinking was by design or the result of the compulsions of the situation, the fact is that the Congress Party never attempted thereafter to return to the system of synchronised polls. The political instability over the years has affected both the Centre and States, especially the latter. That made mid-term Assembly polls necessary. Of late the system has gone completely out of control. Now practically every year is an election year, and there is electioneering without any respite. In 1989 there were Lok Sabha elections and elections to the U.P. Assembly. In 1990 several Assemblies went to the polls. In 1991, again, there were Lok Sabha polls as also elections to the U.P. and Tamil Nadu Assemblies.

The next year (1992) was not free from electoral battles either. There was the Punjab Assembly poll and Presidential and Vice-Presidential elections. The demolition of the Babri mosque on December 6, 1992, under the protection of an elected State Government, was a traumatic event. Throughout the next year (1993) people were chiefly concerned about the terrible riots and aggravation of the communal situation. The November 1993 poll cast its long shadow ahead of the event. The administration was paralysed in several States. The States under President's Rule could not take any decisions. Ad hocism ruled supreme. There was tentativeness about all steps. The Centre barely kept itself from being overwhelmed. All this diverted attention from the pressing problems and adversely affected economic growth.

The round-the-year electioneering has other harmful consequences. The administrative expenditure on elections has mounted. Parties also spend more money on elections. Frequent elections spell dependence of politics on black money and give impetus to expansion of the parallel economy. It also means the strengthening of the nexus between politics and crime and generation of illicit money. The past two decades have witnessed a growing criminalisation of public life. A recent survey showed that nearly one-fourth of the U.P. legislators have criminal records. Candidates not only spend vast sums on elections, in the process they also enrich themselves.

The BJP's electoral setback in November 1993 lifted the pall of gloom. The electorate endorsed the imposition of President's rule in Madhya Pradesh and Himachal Pradesh. Even the Rajasthan voters did not disapprove of it. Now the Supreme Court has unanimously held that recourse to Article 356 is justified if the State Governments concerned offer a challenge to the constitutional order and try to subvert secularism and the rule of law as the Sangh Pariwar and its Governments had done in 1992.

But alas! There was no question of the country getting on with the serious economic business or the urgent task of combating insurgency in the North-west and North-east. The Assembly elections in Orissa, Bihar, Gujarat, Maharashtra, Karnataka and Andhra Pradesh have already begun to loom large on the horizon. T.N. Seshan's daily threats and political leaders' bellicose responses do not let us forget even for a moment that this also is an election year.

The opposition which the Congress will be called upon to face in these elections is not primarily the BJP—although in Gujarat it will be a serious contender for power and in Karnataka also it will be an important force—but the regional forces or a party national only in name.

The Janata Dal had become a formidable force in 1989. But within a space of five years, its different factions became five regional parties: Mulayam Singh's Samajwadi Party in U.P., Devi Lal-Chautala's SJP in Haryana and Lalu Prasad Yadav's, Biju Patnaik's and Devegowda-Hegde's virtually independent outfits in Bihar. Orissa and Karnataka respectively. Its State units in Gujarat and Rajasthan merged with the Congress and partly with the BJP respectively. V.P. Singh's call for a federal structure for the Janata Dal only reflects the ground reality.

The BSP is essentially a regional party of U.P., but it is bravely trying to fan out in Punjab, Madhya Pradesh, Gujarat, Andhra Pradesh, Bihar, West Bengal and Maharashtra and other States with varying degrees of success. Kanshi Ram relies on the OBC-SC alliance. In Andhra Pradesh he denounced the Congress as a Reddy-Kamma Party (most Congress Chief Ministers have been Reddys) and the Telugu Desam as a Kamma Party. N.T. Rama Rao belongs to the Kamma caste. Kanshi Ram wants to create hung Assemblies everywhere. This, I fear, is a purely negative policy. It is not a prescription for a comprehensive and constructive policy of creating a society based on egality, freedom and justice.

In Bihar and Orissa the Janata Dal's position is still strong. Biju Patnaik is by no means popular, but the Congress, perhaps, is even less so. However, Mulayam Singh and Kanshi Ram can considerably weaken Lalu Prasad Yadav's position in Bihar and the defection of Kurmis and Kushwahas can bring defeat. The record of Biju and Lalu is dismal in most areas of public policy and so the possibility of negative vote cannot be ruled out.

In Karnataka, Bangarappa has formed a new regional party. There is talk of his making common cause with Kanshi Ram. That would make the poll a stiff four-cornered contest in most of the constituencies. It would thereby enhance political uncertainty.

In Maharashtra the old opposition parties are in decline. But Prakash Ambedkar is trying to build a new force. Kanshi Ram also wants to intervene as a separate entity. Then there is the Shiv Sena. It prospered under the protective umbrella of a succession of Congress Chief Ministers. Big business supported it. Today it is virtually a Government-sponsored terrorist band. It began with the denunciation of South Indians, and later on declared war on Dalits and Muslims. It need not be said that the Muslim fundamentalists and the Shiv Sena thrive on each others' excesses. Currently its relations with the BJP are strained. But despite differences the BJP does not wish to break with Bal Thackeray.

The most spectacular rise in the eighties was that of N.T. Rama Rao's Telugu Desam. The decline of the Communist movement and successive splits within its ranks created a vacuum which the Janata Party or the Vengal Rao Congress were unable to fill. What alienated the Andhra Pradesh voters from the Congress was, I think, the contempt shown by the Centre towards the Chief Ministers. The incessant demand for money and widespread corruption also induced the Andhra Pradesh voters to turn away from the Congress. The politics of defection (N. Bhaskara Rao in 1984) gave a new lease of life to N.T. Rama Rao. After the lacklustre five-year term, power slipped from NTR's hands. Now Rama Rao hopes to return to power. But Kanshi Ram's intervention might upset the traditional calculations.

A study of regional parties underlines the paradox that while an integrated national party is a must for holding this country of vast diversity together, a unitary national party like the Congress with absolute centralised control tends to ignore the legitimate aspirations of the States for autonomous functioning—in party as well as in governmental affairs.

Another factor is the emergence of warlordism and the appeal of egoistic leaders based on community, sect, ethnicity, linguistic solidarity and caste. They thrive on fancied or real popular grievances. Unless the legitimate grievances are removed and the voters also become more discriminating, warlordism will not disappear. I am not at all sanguine, as some academic political scientists and sociologists are, about a loose confederation of regional leaders, with their super egos, coming together to run the country and preserve its unity. I believe the good of the country lies in democratising the functioning of the political parties, compulsory revelation of the sources of their income and curbing the absolute power of the socalled charismatic leaders to choose candidates for the various representative bodies.

20

MULTI-MEMBER BODIES, ELECTION COMMISSION AND THE CONSTITUTION

Our Constitution is a lengthy document. Every thing has been spelt out in it. No authority enjoys absolute and untrammelled powers. Of course ignorant and selfish people glibly talk of sover-eignty. The Parliament is sovereign, some say. The Cabinet is supreme, others say. There are lawyers, for whom litigation is a goldmine, who say that judiciary is the ultimate authority and its power of interpretation has no limit. All this is the sheerest nonsense. In a democracy it is the people, the electorate—and this embraces all those who are 18 years of age or above—which is the real sovereign. The Constitution is the embodiment of the will of our sovereign people. It is a Constitution under which every authority has limited powers and finite jurisdiction.

The Constitution has created many multi-member authorities. They are collectivities. They are expected to function on the basis of a consensus. The consensus is to be reached through discussion. The democratic mode of functioning places a premium on the powers of persuasion. Coercion by the Chief is completely out of place. He cannot ride roughshod over his colleagues.

The most important multi-member body is the Cabinet. The second is the Supreme Court. Then there are the various High Courts. There are the Union and State Public Service Commissions. Then there is the Election Commission which has vested in it the power of "superintendence, direction and control" of the election process.

All these bodies are collective bodies. All have Chiefs at their head. But the powers and mode of functioning of these bodies, and the role of the Chiefs who are at the head of these multi-member bodies, are not the same.

The Council of Ministers constitutes the political executive. It is the most powerful body. But it is responsible to the directly elected Houses of the Union and State Legislatures. The Council of Ministers—at the Centre—has the Prime Minister at its head. *It aids and advises the President and this advice is binding on him in the exercise of his functions.* The Prime Minister is appointed by the President, *but all "other Ministers shall be appointed by the President on the advice of the Prime Minister." "The Ministers hold office during the pleasure of the President" which, as every novice knows, means the Prime Minister. He can require them to resign. And if they do not comply they will be unceremoniously sacked by the President (Article 75).*

Now take the Supreme Court. It consists of a Chief Justice and "of such other judges" as may be fixed by law. The increase in workload led to an increase in the number of judges. At present the maximum number is twenty-five. This was fixed by Act 22 of 1986.

These judges, be it noted, are (a) not appointed on the advice of the Chief Justice; nor (b) can they be removed on the advice of the Chief Justice—no judgement of the Supreme Court, let me emphatically say, can transform Article 124 into Article 75. There is no use talking of the primacy of the Chief Justice. He has administrative duties. These are important. If he is part of the majority in any matter before the Court he can allot the job of delivering the main opinion to a judge of his choice. In the appointment of judges the Chief Justice shall be consulted "with such other judges" of the higher judiciary "as the President may deem necessary". In the appointment of a judge other than the Chief Justice the incumbent Chief Justice "shall always be consulted". *But it is absolutely clear that he cannot nominate his own successor.* Even the retiring Prime Minister—the Chief political executive—cannot dictate to the President who his successor should be. The President may consult him at his discretion. He may ignore the retiring Prime Minister's wishes completely. *The President will only consider whether his choice of the new Prime Minister will enjoy the confidence of the*

Lok Sabha. To be on the safe side, he asks him, after administering him the oath, to seek confidence of the House. This has happened three times, and in the absence of an elected leader with an absolute majority behind him, this practice can be considered well-established. *The judges may write tons of opinions, but nothing will alter the words of the Constitution and nothing will convince me that the Chief Justice of the Supreme Court is in the same position of as the Prime Minister*. In the matter of removal of judges [Article 124(4)] there is no distinction between the Chief Justice and other Justices of the Apex Court. If the Chief dies or retires, other judges don't lose office as the Cabinet members do.

As to the Union Public Service Commission it also is a multi-member body. The Chairman has certain administrative duties which he has to perform. If the office is vacant, then any other member can be appointed by the President to perform these duties. The Chairman again is not like Prime Minister. On his death or resignation the other members don't cease to be members.

Now let us take the Election Commission. A single member Commission is not mandatory. Article 324(2) gives power to the President to appoint "such number of other Election Commissioners as the President may from time to time fix". Of course parliament can make a law to govern these matters. Now certain pertinent things should be noted. *Unlike the Prime Minister, the appointment "of such number of Election Commissioners" is not done on the advice of the Chief Election Commissioner nor can he ask the President to remove them*. But the President, that is the formal political executive, cannot remove an Election Commissioner, because he has done something which is not to the liking of the ruling party. He can do so only if he holds it necessary for safeguarding the purity of the election process. So removal of other Election Commissioners has been made *conditional on the recommendation of the Chief Election Commissioner*. This by no stretch of imagination can be construed to make him a dictator. He can carry on his *routine administrative* duties on his own responsibility. But on all important policy matters he has to carry the other members with him. In Committees the general rule—and a very salutory rule—is to function on the basis of consensus. All major statutory parliamentary Committees—Public Accounts, Estimates and Public Undertakings

—function on this basis. The Chief Election Commissioner, if he is worthy of his post, will provide leadership and guidance and carry the multi-member Commission with him. *Only when all attempts at compromise and consensus fail should voting be resorted to. This is practical wisdom. T.N. Sheshan is doing some very good things. But his high profile, irratic and authoritarian tendencies cannot be encouraged.* If he does not reform his arbitrary ways, Parliament and the Courts will have to step in. He should not exploit the present unstable parliamentary situation. He did not show much independence of spirit under Indira Gandhi and Rajiv Gandhi. He knew they would have kicked him out. *Even on the issue of the Rajya Sabha carpet-baggers he is selective. Why is he singling out only Manmohan Singh. He should direct his regional electoral officers to prosecute S.R. Bommai, Inder Gujral, BJP's Rajgopal and Vishnukant Shastri and also Bharadwaj, Dinesh Singh and other carpet-baggers.* Otherwise I cannot absolve him of playing dirty politics or of vendetta.

In the only judgement delivered on this subject the question of the functioning of the multi-member E.C. has been discussed. Some of the statements in the opinion of J. Sawant especially the comparision between the Election Commission and the Council of Ministers is totally unacceptable. Nevertheless, the operative portion contains sane advice. It can be summarised thus: "It is an acknowledged rule of transacting business in a multi-member body that when there is no express provision to the contrary, the business has to be carried on unanimously. The rule to the contrary such as the decision by majority, has to be laid down specifically by spelling out the kind of majority-whether simple, special, of all the members or of the members present and voting etc. In a case such as that of the Election Commission which is not merely an advisory body but an executive one, it is difficult to carry on its affairs by insisting on unanimous decisions in all matters. Hence, a realistic approach demands that either the procedure for transacting business is spelt out by a statute or a rule either prior to or simultaneously with the appointment of the Election Commissioners or that no appointment of Election Commissioners is made in the absence of such procedure." *I have reservations about the words "prior to or simultaneously". Nevertheless I suggest that the new legislation should follow the above guidelines given by the Apex Court.*

21

ELECTORAL REFORM BILLS : AN ANALYSIS

A special session of parliament has been summoned by the President to meet on 13 June 1994. The purpose presumably is to consider the two Bills on electoral reforms and the Election Commission. From the reports it is clear that there is really no consensus among parties on the main provisions of the Bills. Even the Congress members are in a state of confusion. Although the Ruling Party has an army of Ministers of Parliamentary Affairs they have neither been able to keep in touch with the various opposition groups whose support is vital not only for the passage of the Constitution Amendment Bill but also for the adoption by the Rajya Sabha of the Representation of the People (Amendment) Bill of 1994. These Parliamentary eyes and ears of the Government are out of touch even with the state of opinion in their own Party.

The reasons are not far to seek. *There is virtually no real Cabinet functioning under P.V. Narasimha Rao. The Political Affairs Committee of the Cabinet is a non-functioning body. Important Departments have no Ministers.* Dinesh Singh is my friend and I think he is a lovable man. But he has no business to turn the Council of Ministers into a Sanatorium, especially when practically a new world has come to birth out of the death pangs and final collapse of the Soviet bloc. There is no Think Tank which can give thought to the complex problems, separate the important from the unimportant and the transient, and frame legislation which will not only resolve the difficulties that have arisen but also secure is smooth passage in Parliament.

It is a pity that P.V.N.R. Government has not learnt any lesson from the fiasco of the Religion Bill. The JD (which then had 60 members) was even then a badly fractured party. No representative or leader of that Party could make any commitment on behalf of his Party and even if he had made it, there was no guarantee that he or the Party would have stuck to it. When the Janata Dal became shaky, the Left also started wobbling. I am not at all sure that the Congress has acted wisely in calling this special session. It is unlikely that the Bills would be passed *in their present form*. Like the Religion Bill these two Bills are ill-thought out and ill-drafted. I shall deal here only with some important clauses.

The most objectionable clause in the amendment to the R.P. Act is clause (5) which seeks to remove the residential qualification for the Rajya Sabha elections. *The Upper House of a federal polity represents the constituent units—whether called States or Provinces— and is its essential feature.* If the Government had further strengthened the existing residential qualification and introduced direct elections to the Rajya Sabha on the basis of multi-member constituencies, with cumulative vote—a form of proportional representation—I would have heartily welcomed these amendments. My only quarrel with Sheshan is that he singles out Dr. Manmohan Singh and allows Inder Gujral, S.R. Bommai (JD); Dinesh Singh, Bharadwaj (Congress) and Vishnukant Shastri and Rajgopal (BJP) to go scot free. L.K. Advani who has emerged as a great defender of T.N. Sheshan is the king of carpet-baggers. He got elected to Rajya Sabha from three areas: Delhi, Gujarat and Madhya Pradesh. Currently, he is being prosecuted for falsely declaring himself as "ordinarily resident" in Madhya Pradesh. His application was not only dismissed by the M.P. High Court, it directed that his sponsor also should be charge-sheeted. I make a distinction between public life and private life. I am talking of Advani's public actions. Let him apologise to the nation before presuming to talk of reform and purity of the election process.

Another objectional clause is about the approval of the Centre on the issue of identity cards. Sheshan is, I think, ignoring two important elements involved in his identity card proposal, which, in fact, I do not disapprove. Durable Identity Cards involve finance; and two it will be taken advantage of by *all manner of illegal immigrants* whose number I put at 12 million. A time bound, self-executing programme of, say five to 10 years, for introducing I.Cs., and eliminating illegal immigrants should therefore be evolved.

I would like Independents, who are vitiating the election process, to produce at least 1000 proposers for Lok Sabha and 200 for the Assemblies.

I am totally opposed to State funding of polls unless there is a prior law on democratisation of political parties—present parties are zamindaris—, ensuring two yearly elections and the right of constituency parties to select their candidates at least in 85% cases; and also an effective curb on parallel economy through tax reform and other measures, and suppression of criminalisation of politics which produces *illicit* money, as distinct from the black money, which arises in the productive process.

The Bills contain some good provisions about holding bye-elections within six months, raising the limit for forfeiture of security deposit to 25 per cent of valid votes, and providing statutory sanction for the Code of Conduct, which, I think, should be carefully redrawn.

The most urgent and expenditure-saving reform would be to have compulsory, synchronised elections of all representative bodies from Panchayat-Municipality up to Parliament in the first week of March every five years, dissolution of Assemblies and suspension of local bodies in the intermediate period notwithstanding.

If a multi-member Election Commission. (EC) is appointed in consultation with the Chief Justice and two senior-most judges of the Supreme Court, with defined procedures, it would really be an independent body and can be entrusted with the local elections. The argument of State Autonomy is bogus. The State Governments want to control the local elections and, if possible, rig them and so the charge they levelled at the Rajiv Gandhi Bills was baseless. I don't like consultation with politicians like the Speaker or Opposition leaders in the appointment of the E.C.

The Constitutional Amendment provides for delimitation of constituencies on the basis of the 1991 Census. But why stop there?

Why not abolish the Indira Gandhi amendment to Article 82 altogether? The Scheduled Castes and Scheduled Tribes will thereby gain a couple of seats in the Lok Sabha and some State Assemblies. I am surprised that Kanshiram and Mayavati and the Jharkandis never talk about this grave injustice.

The Government feels that the incorporation of a specific provision relating to the transaction of business in the multi-member Election Commission *in the Constitution itself* would "clarify" the position and facilitate a "more cohesive functioning" of the E.C. But there is, I think, a better alternative, and it should be tried out.

In my opinion the CEC and EC should forestall the Constitution Amendment Bill by agreeing to follow the main points of the Supreme Court decision in the *Danoa vs. the Union of India.* Let them work on the basis of consensus on all policy questions—as distinct from purely administrative matters—and only in rare cases decide them by a majority. Anyway I am not acting a prophet in saying that this Constitutional Amendment in the present shape will not be able to secure approval of this Parliament.

Why then is the Government going through this rigmarole of a special session of Parliament, drafting of the Bills, and "elaborate" consultation with the Opposition groups? A generally knowledgeable source tells me that the Centre is keen on holding elections in Jammu and Kashmir—for, after all, democracy is a safety valve, as the examples of the Soviet Union, Yugoslavia and a Central European State have shown—and the Centre is apprehensive that Sheshan's wayward and arbitrary behaviour would, instead of alleviating the miserable conditions in that State, aggravate it. *If only T.N. Sheshan will remember that the nation's unity is supreme, that every authority has limited powers and that he is not above the law, he can do immense good to the democratic process.* He will also win the support of numberless people like me.

22

RESTRUCTURING THE ELECTION COMMISSION: A PLEA FOR COMMON SENSE

A Special Parliament Session has been called to meet in the second week of June 1994. The main work before it will be to consider and adopt the Bills one of which relates to the amendment of the Constitution and other to the Representation of the People Acts of 1950 and 1951. The Constitutional Bill involves only two major provisions: one relating to changing the basis of the readjustment of territorial constituencies on the basis of 1991 Census. The other and, perhaps, more important provision concerns the functioning of the three-member Election Commission.

The ostensible object of the amendment of the Election Law is to carry out certain electoral "reforms". I have deliberately used the word "ostensible" and put "reforms" in quotes. For it is doubtful whether all the clauses would reform the system. In fact the attempt to change the Section relating to the pre-condition about a Rajya Sabha candidate being "ordinarily resident in the State" is not only regressive in character, but would remove the arch-stone of the Union Legislature and would damage federalism which is held to be a basic feature of the Constitution and therefore unamendable. *It is disgusting that political parties are shamelessly trying to open the Rajya Sabha to a mass invasion by carpet baggers.*

Last time the Law Department played havoc with the Religion Bills by not confining the Bills to (a) communalism in parties' name; (b) communally restrictive membership; and (c) preaching communal hatred through policy, programmes, general propaganda and party activities. This time the Government by tampering with the nature of the Rajya Sabha is ensuring the rejection of the Amendment.

I will deal here chiefly with the modification of Article 324 relating to the Elections and addition of 324 A.

First, I will summarise the views of the Chief Election Commissioner on this issue. Let me state that I readily give him credit for doing many good thing in the cause of the purity of the electoral process. But he mars all his good work by his arrogance, arbitrary ways and megalomania. T.N. Sheshan briefly argues thus: The Constitution does not empower Parliament to lay procedure inside the Commission. The proposed amendments say that the business of the Commission shall be decided by the three members unanimously. If there is no consensus, decisions shall be by a majority. That is what I have questioned in the Supreme Court. The terms and conditions of Service of the CEC cannot be used to prescribe how internal decisions are taken. This matter is *sub judice*. Parliament cannot change the basic structure, and the suggested amendment would result in the abrogation of free and fair elections. The CEC must have executive-legislative-judicial power.[1]

Here I wish to draw attention to the fact that there already exists a judgement of the Supreme Court on these issues, although, I am afraid that most of the ordinary citizens and even some judges are unaware of its existence. In the eyes of some judges there is no distinction whatever between the text of the constitution, Acts of the Legislatures, Rules framed thereunder, Codes of Conduct among political parties, the famous Ten Commandments of the Old Testament, and Vinoba Bhave's eleven *vratas* which he wanted to be observed with humility and absolute resolution. One of them is *brahmacharya*. If there are no distinctions between the aforesaid instruments, even a judge can be hauled up for cohabiting with his wife!

Before turning to the Supreme Court decision of mid-1991 I shall briefly refer to the attitude of the main parties. Prime Minister Rajiv Gandhi had expressed his firm opposition to a multi-member Commission in December 1988. On the other hand the major political parties had demanded the creation of a multi-member Commission after consultation with the Prime Minister, the Chief Justice of India and leaders of opposition (there was at that point no recognised Leader). *The justification for this demand can best be set out in the words of the aforesaid Supreme Court decision: "There is no doubt that two heads are better than one, and particularly when an institution like the Election Commission is entrusted with vital functions, and is armed with uncontrolled powers to execute them, it is both necessary and desirable that the powers are not exercised by one individual, however all-wise he may be."*[2]

In 1989 Rajiv suddenly changed his mind and a multi-member body was created which was abolished by the V.P. Singh Government on 1st January 1990. It is for V.P. Singh to say whether he consulted the Leader of the Opposition—who then existed—and the Chief Justice of India, a procedure the non-Congress Parties themselves had suggested.

A dismissed Commissioner went to the Supreme Court. The question was: What happens if the multi-member Commission does not function smoothly or on the basis of consensus. In fact unless otherwise prescribed all questions are to be decided by a simple majority as is clear from the wordings of Article 100, 189 and 145. Only when special majorities are required the thing is mentioned in the Constitution. Otherwise a simple majority is assumed.

Articles 100 and 189 relating to Legislative Procedure lay down that all questions shall be determined by a majority of those present and voting. Even Article 145 on the Union Judiciary requires delivery of all opinions by the Supreme Court by a majority. I think there is no such specific provision in the Chapter on the High Courts. Can anybody content therefore that all High Court decisions must be by unanimity, and not a simple majority? Like the Legislatures, the higher courts have rule-making powers. The Legislatures, in addition, can make laws. Indira Gandhi had tried to introduce special majority in the higher courts' judgement. But that was repealed by the Government under Morarji Desai. Article 3 even enables the Constitution to be amended by a simple majority in the area of States reorganisation .

On the other hand speakers can be removed only by a *majority of all the then members of the House,* not just by a majority of those present and voting as Articles 94(3) and 189(1) lay down in clear terms. Special majorities are prescribed for the removal of judges of the Supreme Court and High Courts. Article 368 concerning the Constitution Amendment not only requires a special majority but in respect of certain articles also concurrence of half the States. Article 324 does not prescribe any special majority for the multi-member Commission. This is beyond challenge.

If this is challenged, the Parliament has to step in. Article 324 speaks of "any law made by Parliament" in clause (2) and (5). It no where says that the law has to be made "prior to or simultaneously with the appointments of the Election Commissioners" and yet the Court has inserted these words into the Article on its own. Laws are not made for the sake of fun. They have to be made when persons who are supposed to act reasonably and with a modicum of good will refuse to do so. *It was wholly inadmissible for the Judge who wrote the opinion to read into the Constitution words and phrases of his own making, or make pronouncements not germane to the matter, for these create grave difficulties in situations which cannot always be foreseen.*[3]

It would be much better if the Constitution Bench of the Supreme Court summons the CEC and other Commissioners and tells them to evolve a method of consensus. Only in rare cases the EC should decide by a majority. This mode of functioning by consensus is plain common sense, for the second quote from Sawant (J)'s Danoa judgement itself emphasises this.

We have a very unstable parliamentary situation. The Prime Minister has survived for three years. But that's about all. Sheshan is exploiting this parliamentary stalemate. His high profile activities have added to the administrative paralysis.

In this situation a heavy responsibility rests on the Supreme Court. As an ardent believer in judicial independence, I want the judges to be held in high esteem. Erratic behaviour and haphazard decision-making detract from this esteem. One day they take Sheshan to task. The second day they pull up the Andhra Pradesh Chief Minister. Both deny their statements. The public is puzzled. The casualty of this all-round confusion, I am afraid, will be free and fair elections, for the Government's intention is not above board. It would like to control the electoral process if it can. This must not be allowed.[4]

References

1. *T.N. Sheshan's Interview to Blitz*, 28 May 1994; *The Hindustan Times*, 28 May 1994; L.K. Advani supports Sheshan's megalomaniac claims, *The Hindustan Times*, 24 May 1994; The BJP even backed Sheshan's decision on Mulayam Singh which was reversed by the Supreme Court.
2. S.S. Danoa *Versus* Union of India and others, *Judgements Today*, Vol. 3, No. 10, August 5, 1991, pp. 293-306.
3. *Ibid*.
4. The Government ultimately decided to withdraw the Constitution Amendment Bill.

Section IV

POLITICS OF 1994

23

THE BJP AT THE FORKING OF ROADS

It appears that the recent electoral setback has considerably demoralised the top and middle rung leadership of the BJP. The BJP leaders and their apologists have been assuring their ranks that the BJP's defeat is more apparent than real and that the Party has actually grown in strength and has succeeded in widening its base. I am reminded of the situation in the Socialist Party more than forty years ago. After the First General Election many leaders of the Party became thoroughly disheartened and their demoralisation inevitably affected the rank and file Socialists also. Of course some of those disheartened leaders tried to conceal their disappointment, and bravely talked of the large popular vote which the Party had won in the first trial of strength itself. One leader (Asoka Mehta) even wrote a little book: *The Political Mind of India* with a wealth of statistics. Unfortunately the effort did not even convince the writer who told me in 1952 that it was not possible to beat the Congress in a direct contest, and ways and means would have to be found of working out an accommodation with it.

The demoralisation of leaders is a subjective phenomenon. It arises out of the high expectations cruelly belied. If high expectations are entertained by the leaders, and if they are not fulfilled, no amount of reasoning and statistical data would help them in preserving the morale of the organization. Asoka Mehta, Ramnandan Mishra, Jayaprakash Narayan had high hopes about the outcome of the poll. There was talk of forming Governments in a couple of States. When the Party was beaten, its more than 10 per cent all-India share in the popular vote—a figure which was never surpassed by the Jan Sangh or the Communists or the

Swatantra Party—it was only surpassed by the BJP in 1989—was not able to overcome the leaders' state of depression.

The same thing seems to have happened in the BJP now. For more than two years, that is after the 1991 Lok Sabha poll, the JS-BJP leadership was so elated by its success—it had become the recognised Official Opposition in the Lok Sabha and in the Rajya Sabha, too, it captured the coveted post soon—that its leaders began to say: "Non-Congressism is dead! It is now the BJP versus the rest"!

I also remember how some Socialists had become so frightened by the momentory and dazzling success of the Communists in some States and their 30 seats in the Lok Sabha in 1952 that they had begun to talk of the need for an anti-Communist front! Soon after the June 1991 poll, former Chief Minister of Karnataka, Ram-krishna Hegde, began to preach the virtues of an alliance with the Congress. He testified that the Congress was pure like the Ganga, and even if lakhs of sinners like him took a dip in its holy waters it would remain pure. Surprisely, he was momentarily backed by V.P. Singh, who issued a call for an anti-BJP secular front! That V.P. Singh's Party rejected his suggestion is another matter. The important thing is that he put forward the proposal. An unexpected defeat shatters the self-confidence of faint-hearted leaders who are only used to ride waves of popular approval. The BJP leaders and their followers are not the ones who can face adversity calmly. We know the devices they invented to keep out of jail on parole or obtain release through apology letters in 1975-77.

The BJP's cry in the November mini-general election was: "*Aaj Panch Pradesh, kal sara Desh.*" First we will capture all the five States, next we will capture the Centre. L.K. Advani was the inventor of the Rathayatra. It had clicked in 1990. He became the Leader of the Opposition, with the status of a Cabinet Minister in June 1991. He had successfully pushed A.B. Vajpayee to the background. Everybody in the BJP and the Press was singing his praises. He himself behaved as if he was poised to take oath on the morrow. He had gathered around him a team of modernist PRO experts. Money was no problem. Carried away by their own enthusiasm the RSS *Pariwar* decided at the highest level to demolish the Babri

Mosque and thus pave the road to central power. They completely misread the public mood. An average Hindu does not relish destruction of religious shrines no matter of which faith. When they returned to Delhi Advani was faced with a hostile reaction. He tried to dissociate himself from the act of vandalism by resigning as Leader of the Opposition. This was not an act of courage. Having done nothing to stop the vandals at Ayodhya, he now wanted to disclaim responsibility. Bal Thakerey was more candid and courageous in accepting the responsibility for the act. The BJP was saved from the *potentially* embarrassing situation by the Janata Dal's ridiculous demonstration in Parliament on 7 December 1992. Instead of getting Parliament to pass a motion condemning the act, it disrupted the proceedings. The Prime Minister also, by rashly promising to construct the mosque on the same site, rescued the BJP from public opprobrium. The farce of arrests and release of the BJP leaders also helped the BJP to regain its confidence.

The dismissal of the BJP Government had really evoked little mass protest. For everybody knew that the resources of all three BJP Governments had been mobilised for getting volunteers to Ayodhya and destroying the structure. The indifference of the people in HP, MP and UP was quite striking. That should have alerted the Party's leadership. But they remained self-hypnotised for nearly a year. Other Parties' mistakes made the BJP very complacent.

When the dates of the Assembly polls were announced the Party, which was in a state of intoxication, launched a high profile propaganda. The BJP had planted its men in the Press in the previous fifteen years; it had also won over new converts. The Press, especially the Hindi press, was quite favourable to the BJP. The BJP leaders' expectations soared skywards. Seeing the former Janata factions at loggerheads, the BJP was quite confident that it would sweep the polls. From the euphoric L.K. Advani to sober A.B. Vajpayee everybody was talking of the collapse of the Narasimha Rao Government and the imminent mid-term Lok Sabha poll.

It is against these mounting expectations that we have to view the impact of the poll verdict on the BJP. The BJP has really no convincing explanation for its defeat in MP and HP. There the

Janata Dal or other parties did not matter. The BSP of Kanshi Ram, if anything, hurt the Congress, and not the BJP. *But the Sunderlal Patwa and Shanta Kumar administrations were so unpopular that the voters rejected them.* The pro-BJP scribes had written off Rajasthan, and yet the seasoned Bhairon Singh Shekhawat performed much better than the other Chief Ministers. In Delhi the fact that the BJP was not in power helped; also beneficial to the BJP was the ineffective intervention of the Janata Dal and the decision of the Sikhs to vote for the BJP. The role of some Delhi Congress leaders in the 1984 riots is so notorious that I am not at all surprised that the Sikhs in Delhi plumped for the BJP.

Much of the trouble the BJP is facing today is due to the fact that it has now become a big party. It is a large multi-State party, though not a national party in the sense the Congress is a national party. In Madhya Pradesh although it did not win, its share of the popular vote was 38.7 per cent; it sustained a loss of only one per cent. The Congress gain of 7 per cent was at the expense of the JD and other smaller parties. In HP the BJP got 36.2 per cent vote, a loss of over 5.5 per cent. In UP it managed to garner 33.3 per cent vote, *two per cent higher than in 1991. Its performance in Rajasthan was commendable. Its vote went up from 29.4 to 38.6 per cent, a gain of more than nine per cent.* The JD voters swung to the BJP banner. But all this is poor consolation for the BJP. The loss of three State Governments and the dashing of the hope of an early assumption of power at the Centre is very galling for the BJP. The exhilaration produced by Jai Shri Ram had so far curbed and concealed the seething contradictions within the Party: supporters of Hindutva and temple demolition versus those who believe in a comprehensive socio-economic programme; the upper castes vs. the OBCs, Harijans and Adivasi; *Swadeshi* vs. globalisation and liberalisation; the simple and austere RSS living styles against the ostentatious consumerism of the BJP elite; big capitalists and MNCS versus the small trader; the middlemen bania versus the peasants; and, finally, one power group against the other in practically all important State units.

The RSS General Secretary, H.V. Sheshadri, it appears, has reservation about the BJP's panicky reaction to the election results as evidenced by its hanging Dr. Ambedkar's portrait alongside of the Shambuk-killer Ram's and its going in for "backwardism". Sheshadri said the RSS was against casteism and was not influenced by political or electoral considerations. It was not bothered about the BSP type politics. So far the RSS leaders had the last word in the BJP politics. But the politicians and legislators, actuated by the insatiable lust for power and desire to grow rich quickly—and their number is quite large in the BJP—will not be amenable in future to the centralised control of the RSS. *The BJP leaders and ranks are not only demoralised, they are utterly confused and do not know in which direction to go.* The Bharatiya Janata Party and the Sangh Pariwar are truly at the forking of roads. It remains to be seen which road the saffron caravan eventually decides to take.

24

IS THE CONGRESS IN IRREVERSIBLE DECLINE?

The Congress has been one of the world's most enduring political parties. It was established to foster national unity and secure introduction of democratic institutions in our country. It soon became the chief vehicle of India's national aspirations and a potent instrument of the struggle for freedom. It was largely Mahatma Gandhi who transformed it into a formidable mass organisation. It was often compared with Lenin's Bolshevik Party. Both were revolutionary parties, but after the revolution both changed themselves into ruling parties. Lenin's Party captured power by revolutionary means, Gandhi's Party received power from British hands peacefully. It was the receipient of power because it was without question the most representative organisation of the Indian people. Both parties, when they got the levers of power into their hands, sought to wield that power to consolidate the new state and bring about the socio-economic changes which they held to be necessary for their own country's survival and progress. But here the comparison ends. While Lenin's Party proceeded to establish one-party rule—Lenin even banned the working class and peasant parties like the Mensheviks and Social Revolutionaries—the Congress Party framed a democratic constitution, allowed other parties to function and gave them an opportunity to try to win popular support at the periodically held free and fair elections. There is thus a basic difference between the one-party rule established by force (the USSR) and the one-party dominant system (India) which was the result of the democratic process. The Mahatma had built the Congress Party on a firm and sound foundation. It had branches and supporters in the remotest part of the country and under him the Party had to its credit such a glorious record of service that despite the vicissitudes of time and the inevitable degenerative processes, it has survived for more than 108 years. Lenin's Party, which enjoyed an absolute power monopoly, has virtually disappeared, but the Congress which forced itself to compete with other parties on an equal footing has not only managed to survive, but is still in power at the Centre. It has successfully faced several challenges in the past two-and-half years, has falsified newspaper forecasts of its rout and has even put together—by hook or by crook—a majority of its own in the Lok Sabha.

The Prophets of Doom, however, refuse to be silenced. They are predicting the Congress Party's disintegration and eventual death. I therefore propose to analyse in perspective the shifts in public opinion and voting patterns that have taken place over a period of time and hazard a prognosis.

In the first fifteen years after the first General Election organised on the basis of universal suffrage, the dominance of the Congress was attested by its large popular vote and even larger majority in Parliament. Its vote was between 44 to 47 per cent. This gave it a two-thirds majority in the first three Lok Sabhas. Towards the end of this period Jawaharlal Nehru died, and he was succeeded by Lal Bahadur Shastri, whose early death led to the installation of Indira Gandhi as Prime Minister in 1966. The CPP, in a contested election, rejected Morarji Desai as the Party's standard bearer and chose Mrs. Gandhi. The 1967 election reduced the Congress vote to 40.80 per cent. Its large majority in the Lok Sabha was slashed, but it still had a clear majority over all the other parties combined. The split in the Congress (1969) and Indira's vast facelift operation brought surprising results. The Congress under her stewardship secured in the 1971 Lok Sabha election 43.7 per cent vote and, again, two-thirds seats. But the atrophy of internal democracy and dynastic politics in the Congress put the democratic institutions themselves in grave jeopardy, and the voters wreaked their vengeance on the Congress in 1977. Its vote fell to 34.5 per cent—an all-time low—and its representation in the Lok Sabha was reduced to 154. Again there was a split in the Congress in 1978, but it was more than balanced by the break-up of the Janata Party more than a year later. The seventh General Election once again gave the Congress a two-thirds majority on a 42.7 per cent vote. The sharp division in the non-Congress vote accounted for this unsurprising result. The 1984-85 election was an abnormal affair, it was dominated by the tragedy of Indira Gandhi's assassination. *It was really her posthumous victory which gave Rajiv Gandhi a plurality of 48.1 per cent—the highest ever—with the unprecedented 415 seats out of 517.*[1] (Some seats could not be filled, for Assam could not complete its poll) Some sychophants ascribed this astonishing Congress performance to Rajiv Gandhi's charisma. But this was not so. For Rajiv Gandhi, though well meaning, soon proved that he was a loser. He lost the polls in Punjab, Assam, West Bengal, Haryana and Kerala within two or three years.

In 1987-88 the Congress Government was rocked by the Bofors and Submarine scandals. V.P. Singh combined with the Lok Dal and Janata Party to launch a new party and a new political formation—the Janata Dal and the National Front. The period from 1980 to 1989 had been disastrous for the Congress. Indira Gandhi appeared to have lost her old decisiveness. Sanjay Gandhi's death shattered her, although outwardly she showed herself fully in command of the Party and the Government. But she was unable to control the communal situation in UP and the riots in Moradabad and Meerut in the early eighties shook the confidence of the Muslim minority in the Congress. Indira Gandhi also dithered on the issue of Sikh terrorism in Punjab. She allowed the terrorists to accumulate arms and make Harmandir Sahib their bastion. The ill-conceived Blue Star operation—the deft handling of Hazaratbal in Srinagar provides a pleasant contrast—alienated the Sikhs, a considerable section of which had in the past supported the Congress in Punjab. Elsewhere, that is outside Punjab, the Sikhs had always backed the Congress as against other parties. Rajiv Gandhi and his new team of advisers, headed by the likes of Arun Nehru, committed blunder after blunder. They split the National Conference in Jammu and Kashmir, removed Farookh Abdulla and installed Gul Mohammad Shah as Chief Minister. They thereby paved the way for insurgency in J & K. They dismissed N.T. Rama Rao and in the process weakened the Congress in Andhra Pradesh. In Karnataka the Congress had to pay dearly for the Gundu Rao interlude. With Devraj Urs forming a regional party of his own, the Congress position was undermined in Karnataka also. Although Devraj Urs passed away, the Janata Party stepped into his shoes and assumed power in the State. Not only N.T. Ram Rao soon triumphantly returned to power, he won a massive mandate in 1985. R.K. Hegde, who adroitly dissolved the Assembly, also managed to win an absolute majority in the Karnataka Assembly in the same year.

Acute factionalism in Karnataka and Andhra Pradesh vividly illustrates the Congress predicament. In 1977 when large parts of India rejected Indira Gandhi, the South had stood by her. With the help of its allies the Congress had been successful both in Kerala and Tamil Nadu also. But its 1977 victory in Karnataka and Andhra Pradesh, secured purely on its own strength, was truly spectacular. It had polled 56.8 and 57.4 per cent votes in the two States respectively! The Congress after its debacle in 1983 and 1985 had of course recovered its lost position in Karnataka in 1989 and in Andhra Pradesh in 1991. But these last few years have not been happy years for the Congress. Groupism is eating into the vitals of the Congress in these two States. It was after making these two States the base that Indira Gandhi had launched her successful bid to recapture the Centre in 1978-79. If it is defeated in these two states, its hold on central power would become even more precarious.

The UP Congress, with the blessings of Rajiv Gandhi, Arun Nehru and Buta Singh adopted in the mid-eighties a policy of appeasing the Hindu communalists by playing up the Ayodhya issue. They got the locks removed on the Babri Masjid gate. This was a signal for launching a powerful movement. The UP Congress Chief Minister made an agreement with the Vishwa Hindu Parishad and blessed the Shilanyas. Rajiv Gandhi even announced—in a curious move—that the establishment of Ram Rajya was the goal of Congress policy. Rajiv obviously did not have Mahatma Gandhi's moral order in view. The object was to show that not the BJP-VHP-RSS, but only the Congress could realise the Hindu dream of Ram Rajya. The tactics did not pay. The Congress Party appeared to abandon the middle path and lost both ways. The formation of the Janata Dal, with its appeal to the OBCs, minorities and Scheduled Castes, further isolated the Congress and the elections to the Lok Sabha and to the UP Assembly in 1989 saw a precipitate fall in the illusory Congress strength as reflected in the post-Indira Gandhi assassination Lok Sabha elections.

The Congress loss threatens to be permanent in UP and Bihar. The Muslims and Harijans began to desert the Congress in the eighties. Unlike in the South, the Congress in the North, dominated by the Upper Castes, had disdained to woo the OBC's, a substantial chunk of the population. The Congress leaders of UP and Bihar rejected the Kalelkar Commission Report and refused to introduce reservation for the OBCs—a major plank of the Southern Congress. The OBCs gravitated towards the SSP (sixties) and (BKD plus the SSP) and the Lok Dal in the seventies and eighties. The Janata Dal also learned heavily on the intermediate castes, the OBCs and the Muslims. Kanshiram's BSP also was slowly gathering strength as a party of the Dalits and the OBCs. In the Ninth Lok Sabha elections, the long standing Congress majority at the Centre became a thing of the past. For Congressmen this was a very painful experience. It polled 39.53 per cent votes as against 17.79 of the JD, 11.30 of the BJP, 6.55 of the CPI-M and 2.57 per cent of the CPI. The total of the votes of the latter four parties was still a little less than that of the Congress-I. It was the avoidance of multi-lateral contests as a result of non-Congress unity that had led to a sharp fall in the seats won by the Congress. Nevertheless the Congress led by Rajiv Gandhi was still the largest party, though the Janata Dal, the Left and the BJP together enjoyed a clear majority in the Lower House. The BJP which had been apparently eclipsed in 1985, reemerged with new strength in 1989, "invigorated" both by its electoral alliance with the Janata Dal and also by the Ayodhya issue which had been "ripened" for it by the RSS *Pariwar* in 1980s. The BJP's 89 seats in the Lok Sabha showed that the Congress attempt to woo the Hindu Vote Bank had failed miserably. The BJP grew at the expense of the Congress in UP.

The V.P. Singh interlude proved disastrous from every point of view. The edifice which the Janata Dal had created collapsed. The Janata Dal disintegrated and with that its factions lost power in Rajasthan, Haryana, Gujarat and Uttar Pradesh.

V.P. Singh prided himself on his ability to manage contradictions—not resolve them. But these contradictions blew up his Party and his Government. There was an unparallelled surge of communal feeling and a considerable section of the electorate became infected with the poison. Rajiv's reluctance to face the electorate induced him to put Chandra Shekhar in power, but this did not help much. When the inevitable Lok Sabha elections were held in May-June 1991—they were disrupted by Rajiv Gandhi's assassination—both the Congress and the BJP profited by the break-up of the Janata Dal. The over-all popular vote of the Congress went down from 39.5 per cent to 36.5 per cent, but the number of seats it won however jumped. The BJP vote rose from 11.3 per cent to 20 per cent and the number of seats went up from 89 to 119. The Janata Dal's vote as well as seats fell. From 144 seats in the Ninth Lok Sabha the number now was below 60. The division of vote between V.P. Singh and Mulayam Singh was so sharp that the BJP not only won 50 out of UP's 85 Lok Sabha seats, it captured the Uttar Pradesh Assembly also.

Elated by the BJP's success L.K. Advani acted as if he was about to take oath as Prime Minister. Earlier he had said, "let the Governments complete their full terms, they will be judged by their performance." But the Sangh *Pariwar* was not prepared to wait. All its organizations and Governments resolved to challenge the constitutional order and demolished the Babri mosque in defiance of the Court orders and cynical violation of solemn assurances. The four BJP Governments were dismissed. For one whole year the country witnessed a very high profile BJP propaganda. But when the test came in the November 1993 mini-general election, the BJP failed. It lost badly in MP and HP. In UP it was unable to win a majority. But the election was not a total rout for the BJP, for it improved its position in Rajasthan and captured the Delhi Assembly.

The demoralisation in the BJP is proportionate to its vaulting pre-election ambitions and hopes. All the suppressed contradictions and group conflicts have now surfaced with redoubled force. M.M. Joshi has launched a subtle campaign against Advani. The BJP OBCs and SCs are demanding their share. To appease them some are talking of social engineering. The BJP spokesmen are arguing that the BJP has not lost, it has really gained, for taking all the Assemblies together it has polled more votes than the Congress. One pro-BJP journalist wrote that "the BJP polled 38.10 per cent of the total votes in four States and Delhi. This figure is way above the 26.24 per cent tally of the Congress and 16 per cent recorded by the SP-BSP combine and 9.08 per cent of the Janata Dal". Apart from the reliability of these unofficial figures, these figures have to be balanced against the Assembly election results of 1991. Seven Assemblies and one Union Territory had gone to the polls then.In terms of official figures the Congress secured 24.83, the BJP 14.36, the JD 7.32 and the CPI-M 12.96 per cent votes. The next trial of strength will come in November 1994 and early 1995, when Orissa, Bihar, Gujarat, Maharashtra, Andhra Pradesh—and also Karnataka—will elect new Assemblies. The prospects of the Congress in these States, as of today, do not look bright. In the Prime Minister's own State, the Telugu Desam is showing signs of revival, and it is likely to wrest power from the Congress. The loss of power in Andhra Pradesh would be a blow to the Prime Minister's prestige, although it may not affect his continuance in power. As to the BJP, it will also not perform better than in November 1993. It will concentrate on Gujarat and try to maintain its unexpected 1991 advance in Karnataka. But it cannot expect a bonanza in Bihar, Orissa, Maharashtra and Andhra Pradesh. *The overall impression will be one of stalemate.* In June 1996 will come the Lok Sabha elections. The Congress has ample time to put its own house in order, to stimulate the economy and win back at least some sections of the alienated groups till it finally faces the crucial 1996 challenge. The Congress has shown enough resilience in the past and can do so again. The strength of the Congress lay in its being national. It did not belong to any region, although its programme of reorganization of States gave the various regions, the opportunity to grow. The Congress was not sectional. But it enabled the neglected strata to realise their aspirations, through reservation of seats for the SCs and STs in the Legislatures and reservation for them and the OBCs in the services. It was not a class party. It is not controlled by any one class. It represents several classes, although the CPI-M denounces it as a bourgeois-landlord party. It was also not communal. It belonged to people of all faiths.

It is true that the Congress as Party and Government did not foster work ethic among the people or encourage entrepreneurship, *but in its best days it did care about the poor and the lowly.* It was the Mahatma and the Congress which gave the people adult franchise, a right which the British people took almost a century to win. It is this right which the OBCs, the Dalits and the Adivasis are today using effectively to assert themselves. Insofar as the Congress deviated from these principles and allowed itself to be exploited by the vested interests and upper caste coteries, it stultified itself. To the extent it departed from the high standards of probity and integrity, it fell in popular esteem.

The greatest weakness of the Congress is the money-making madness that has seized its Ministers and legislators. They are totally enmeshed in the crassest form of materialism. This desire to grow rich quickly has made them the patrons and protectors of musclemen and mafias. The Congress cannot regain its previous popular approval unless Congressmen's insatiable appetite for riches is curbed. Some Ministers and legislators have to be made examples. Unless they are punished for wrong-doing, there will be no improvement in the administration. If there is corruption at the top, nobody can eliminate it at the bottom. If a question is asked as to what is coming in the way of India's rapid economic advance the answer is corruption at all levels of the Government. Remove that, control the population growth and prosperity will be within the reach of the common people. The Congress has renewed itself often, and can renew itself again, if it can recapture even a small portion of the spirit which the Mahatma had put into it in those magic years.

The Socialists, the Communists, Kripalani's KMPP, the Swatantrites, Morarji's Congress, the Jan Sangh, the Janata Dal and many others have time and again forecast the Congress Party's early demise. Yet by some quirk of history most of these groups have gone into the oblivion or are about to go into the oblivion. But astoundingly the battered Congress continues to live. Despite the desperate straits to which it has been reduced, it is still not wise to pronounce the sentence: "Irreversible decline and early death"!

25

DENIZEN OF THE WORLD OF MAKE-BELIEVE

The Janata Dal is fast becoming an object of ridicule. It has reduced itself to a truly pitiable condition. Only four or five years ago it was a bright star in the political firmament. It appeared that it would fill the space left empty by the shrinking of the Congress-I strength under Rajiv Gandhi. It won 144 constituencies in the 1989 Lok Sabha elections. With the help of the Left Front and the BJP it formed the Government. Its performance in UP and Bihar was extremely impressive. When the BJP entered into a friendly contest with it in some UP constituencies—outside the electoral adjustments mutually agreed to—it was badly mauled by the JD. In the Assembly elections also it did well. While the BJP was able to form one-party Ministries in Madhya Pradesh and Himachal Pradesh, the two largest States of UP and Bihar fell into JD's lap as also Orissa. In Haryana it already had a two-thirds majority. There were coalition Ministries in Rajasthan and Gujarat, the first was headed by the BJP and the second by the JD.

If V.P. Singh is to be given the credit for putting the JD in the centre of the Indian political stage—and this cannot be denied to him—its subsequent marginalisation has also to be attributed largely to his personality.

V.P. Singh has within his own person what one famous writer, T.B. Macaulay, in a picturesque phrase, called "a grotesque assemblage of incongrous qualities". He was known as a man of financial probity. Nobody really questioned his personal honesty despite the clumsy attempts to malign him. But that does not mean that he is not devious in other matters. Some strange inner compulsion of his personality drives him to play, like some silver screen actors, a double role: that of a power politician and that of a Messiah of "the poor and the lowly". This impels him to make duplicitous statements about his non-attachment to power and office. Five years ago he started by saying that he will not contest the Allahabad bye-election unless Amitabh Bacchan was the candidate. He quickly ate his own words. Next he said he did not wish to be Prime Minister. He did not stick to his statement. He not only became Prime Minister, but achieved this office, *for no reason,* by clumsy circuitous methods. In 1989 he would have easily won the Leadership of the JD Parliamentary Party in a democratic election. But he had recourse to deviousness to outwit Chandra Shekhar and avoid a contest. He proposed Devi Lal for Leader. Devi Lal was unanimously declared elected. Devi Lal kept the bargain. He immediately declined and offered the Leadership to V.P. Singh, who accepted it with a great show of false modesty. That the members were stunned by the proceedings was obvious. Chandra Shekhar naturally felt cheated. The other half of the dirty bargain was to make Devi Lal Deputy Prime Minister and his son, Omprakash Chautala, Chief Minister of Haryana. This had predictable consequences and within eight months V.P. Singh and Devi Lal fell out.

Towards the end of 1993 V.P. Singh had, in a meaningless exercise begun hawking the high offices of the state and the party. He first offered Presidentship of the Republic to a Harijan and Adivasi, and chose to break with the Left on this issue. He continued to offer other offices to his colleagues and friends. He offered Lalu Yadav Prime Ministership at a time when the number of JD MPs was going down. Lalu swallowed the bait and launched a high profile election campaign in November last year! Now he has offered Deve Gowda Chief Ministership of Karnataka, a State where his own influence is negligible. He also offered Party Presidentship to "Christian George Fernandes". Few days ago S.R. Bommai and Lalu Yadav told the JD Executive that V.P. Singh was not averse to assuming the office himself. When V.P. was Prime Minister, for the Rajya Sabha he picked up only members of the forward class! And yet surprisingly V.P. Singh's followers claim that he is the Prophet of social justice. But in his previous career he had never championed the cause of the OBCs, SCs and STs. It was as a weapon of factional struggle that the Mandal report was used by him. But now V.P. Singh donned the Prophet's mantle made no attempt to work out a consensus and, in the process, alienated the BJP and lost the Confidence Motion. The Party broke up. First V.P. fought Devi Lal, then Mulayam Singh and, finally, Ajit Singh. All this affected the electoral fortunes of the JD.

Let us first take a look at the results of the Ninth and Tenth Lok Sabha elections. In Bihar the JD vote fell from 37.66 to 34.14 per cent—a little over three per cent. In UP it came down from 35.90 per cent in 1989 to 21.65 per cent in 1991. Orissa also registered a decline. In Karnataka there was a drop of rearly 10 per cent, from 28.34 to 18.47 per cent. In Rajasthan the fall was precipitate: from 25.68 per cent to 6.16 per cent. In Haryana and Gujarat it was wiped out.

Did the JD draw any lesson from this set back? No. It continued its faction warfare. In the bye-elections held in UP after the Lok Sabha poll, V.P. Singh spent most of the time in Amethi, campaigning for his candidate against Satish Sharma. What was the result? The JD candidate lost his security deposit. This produced no impact on the JD. The bickering in fact intensified. In November 1993 came the mini-general election. The Janata Dal's losses in this important battle were 9.81 in MP, 17.8 in Rajasthan, 3.87 in HP and in the crucial State of UP its vote fell from 18.84 per cent in 1991 to 12.33 per cent in November 1993. In terms of seats, the number came down from 91 seats to 27 seats.

Within a space of four years there has taken place a complete transformation of the position of the JD in the political spectrum. Every rational individual thought that if the JD had done badly in 1991, it had down worse in the Assembly elections in November 1993. But not so the JD's topmost leader, Vishwanath Pratap Singh. He lives in a self-created world. So do his admirers and supporters. For them the question of self-introspection does not arise. It is no use talking to them about the self-inflicted wounds. For they see no wounds. They do not think they have been rejected. Have not millions observed them telling Pranay Roy and Vinod Dua that they had not lost and that it was really their victory. They have since repeated these statements in press briefings and news conferences.

Some days ago an old Janata Dal worker from Uttar Pradesh came to see me and recited to me some verses of Poet Bacchan—Amitabh's father. I have forgotten most of them, but two lines have remained etched in my memory. The idea is as old as Hinduism for there is also a verse in Sanskrit conveying the same meaning. The Bacchan lines were: *Kisi Murti par pushpa chadha tu, Pooja meri ho jati hai.* You may place your flowers at the feet of any idol, the worship performed is my worship.

People argued that in UP the JD had been routed. In V.P. Singh's own district of Allahabad, where the JD held eight seats in the dissolved Assembly and where Lalu Yadav campaigned vigorously, the JD lost each and every seat to Kanshi Ram's BSP. Its overall performance also was dismal. But V.P. Singh's followers say that the victory of Kanshi Ram and Mulayam Singh is only apparent, not real. The victory is V.P. Singh's, for it was he who championed the cause of social justice.

If you say the Congress won in MP and HP, V.P. Singh's men would correct you immediately, and say that the Congress-I success is only an outward one. V.P. Singh being the real Messiah of secularism, if the election results are analysed *in depth*, it will be clear that it is V.P. Singh's policy which has won a notable triumph in the traditional strongholds of the BJP.

If you argue that the Janata Dal's intervention in Rajasthan and Delhi was pathetic, the V.P. Singh followers would hotly contest the statement. They would say in great amazement: "Why are you being so obtuse? V.P. Singh wanted the Congress-I, which connived at the destruction of the Babri Masjid, to be punished. This is what the Rajasthan and the Delhi voters have done. The Congress-I is out. It is a memorable success of V.P. Singh's political line. *Only the dull-witted cannot penetrate through the veil of illusion to the underlying reality.* It is stupid people who say that the voters have poured libations to the SP-BSP or the Congress-I or the BJP. No! A well known Sanskrit Subhashita says:

So just as all the rivers flow into the great ocean, just as the worship done to the various gods ultimately goes to the One True God—call him what you will, "Keshava" or "Shankara"—, similarly the votes apparently cast for other parties are really votes given to our great "Vishwanath". It is purely a matter of discernment"!

After his return from abroad, where he had gone for medical treatment, people expected, on the basis of the assurances given by Lalu Yadav that V.P. Singh would accept the Presidentship of the Janata Dal, which S.R. Bommai had literally been forced to relinquish. But this did not happen. Bommai has again declared that he would continue as President till a new one is elected.[1]

For weeks together V.P. Singh has been having recourse to a curious method of regaining public sympathy. He is holding news conferences and giving press interviews of which the main theme is his illness. It would not be an exaggeration to say that he has been wearing his illness on his sleeves and hawking it around the country. When some of my Socialist friends like Madhu Dandavate, in a display of unbecoming flattery, compare him to Jayaprakash Narayan, I feel humiliated. The Socialist leaders were a noble, self-sacrificing group. Yusuf Meherally was ill for long years. But he never talked about it publicly. Acharya Narendra Deva did not give press interviews about the state of his health. JP was on dialysis for 48 months. But he never harped on it publicly to gain sympathy.

Newspaper Editors and politicians deceived themselves when they called him "grand master of the political chess," or a great vote getter. His vote getting capacity was put to the test thrice after June 1991. He stayed in Amethy for a fortnight and his candidate lost his security deposit in the bye-election. Then he campaigned in some places in UP in November 1993. It made no impact. The Messiah of social justice went to Vaishali and donned the Rajput war robes (*Kesaria*, figuratively speaking). But that also made no difference to the outcome of the poll.

On most issues—liberalisation, Election Commission, policy towards the BSP and Mulayam Singh's SP—his statements are absolutely confusing. With such a leader the Janata Dal needs no enemies.

References

1. On 21 June 1994 there was another split in the Janata Dal. V.P. Singh called the new division "logical". The real driving force behind this fission was the dissatisfaction of a large group, headed by Nitish Kumar against Lalu Yadav, Chief Minister of Bihar.

26

WHY DO REGIONAL PARTIES ENDURE?

Quite a few Regional Parties arose regularly on the eve of elections and disappeared into the limbo after some years. The cause of the splits was in the State Congress Organizations and distribution of tickets. It was never ideological differences. We had the Democratic Congress (1951), Bangla Congress, Utkal Congress, Maharashtra Samajvadi Congress, Karnataka Congress and so on. Nobody remembers them. Bangarappa has again formed a party taking the old name Karnataka Congress. Devraj Urs had also formed a Karnataka Congress in 1979. But it merged in the K.B. Reddy-Y.B. Chavan Congress and Urs became the latter's President. But Urs did not abide there. He preferred a regional role and set up his Kranti Ranga. Bangarappa was a member of this new Party. After Urs's sudden death, Kranti Ranga joined the Janata Party. In the 1983 Assembly elections the Janata Party emerged as the largest Party. However the Lingayat-Vokkaliga leaders were hostile to Bangarappa. They also did not agree on the name of Deve Gonda (Vokkaliga) or Bommai (Lingayat). They chose as Chief Minister R.K. Hegde—after some manipulation by Biju Patnaik and other Central observers. The Telangana Samiti in the seventies was dominated by members of the Congress,—although there was a sprinkling of Socialists—and after some time most of its members like Chenna Reddy rejoined the Congress. The North-east India, including Assam and Sikkim, has seen the rise and fall of many regional parties. The only common trait they share was their volatility.

The Swatantra Party was an amalgamation of various regional groups, including Orissa's Ganatantra Parishad. That Party dominated opposition politics in Gujarat, Rajasthan, Bihar and Orissa and also at the Centre in the sixties and then it evaporated. President Ranga again joined the Congress, Minoo Masani retired from poli-tics, and Piloo Mody merged in the Lok Dal.

The Lok Dal too was a combination of the regional group in Haryana and a substantial section of the former SSP in UP. The Lok Dal later merged in the Janata Dal. The Janata Dal is in the process of disintegration since 1990, with Mulayam Singh forming his own Socialist Party and Ajit Singh joining the Congress with his rump following. The JD's Devi Lal faction flaunts the SJP label.

With the recent decline of the Congress, Regional parties have come to play an important role in our public life. There have been both ephemeral and durable regional formations. We need not overmuch concern ourselves here with some of the aforesaid ephemeral parties most of which were the off shoots of the Congress.

The CPI-M may flaunt day in and day out, its internationalism, but it is not a national party, not even a real multi-State party. It is a confederation of two regional parties: Jyoti Basu's Bhadraloka-dominated Party of the Bengali-speaking areas and EMS-Nayanar's Kerala Party. There are a dozen or so miniscule leftist parties in West Bengal, but they are like parasites on the CPI-M. Over vast areas of the country the CPI-M is virtually non-existent. In Kerala, a highly literate State, the politics is fragmented. There are several floating parties based on community, religious sect and caste. They form alliances with the two dominant parties—the Congress or the CPI-M—to run the Government. The CPI-M has been passing resolutions about intensifying its work in the Hindi-speaking States for nearly three decades. But neither in these States nor in the Western India States of Gujarat and Maharashtra the CPI-M or the CPI has been able to create a mass base.

The Hindi-speaking States and Western India have not taken kindly to Regional parties. In this vast stretch the parties of this kind when formed either had a fleeting life or have had a precarious existence on the periphery of politics—Haryana Vikas Party, the Peasants' and Workers' Party and various Republican factions in Maharashtra.

But the question is are things changing in the Hindi-speaking areas also?

The Janata Dal had become a formidable force in 1989-90. It had assumed office at the Centre with the support of the BJP and the Left. It has formed its own Governments in Haryana, UP, Bihar and Orissa. It was also a partner in the coalitions in Gujarat and Rajasthan. It had a strong presence in Karnataka. But V.P. Singh showed neither the desire nor the capacity to build a national party. And so within two years it broke up. It was wiped out in Gujarat and Rajasthan. Its different factions became four regional parties: Mulayam Singh's Samajvadi Party in UP, Devilal-Chautala's SJP in Haryana and Lalu Yadav and Biju Patnaik's *virtually independent outfits* in Bihar and Orissa respectively. To be candid the prospects of the revival of the JD as a national party or even its becoming the focus of a new confederal set up are nil.

The BSP is essentially a regional party of UP, but it is bravely trying to fan out in Punjab, Madhya Pradesh, Haryana, Andhra Pradesh, Bihar, West Bengal and Maharashtra with varying degrees of success. Kanshi Ram relies on the OBC-SC alliance. It has had some success in UP, Punjab and MP. In Andhra Pradesh he denounces the Congress as a Reddy-Kamma Party (most Congress Chief Ministers have been Reddys) and Telugu Desam as a Kamma Party. N.T. Rama Rao belongs to the Kamma caste. Kanshi Ram wants to create a situation where neither of the two dominant parties would be able to form a Government by itself. This is how he would make the BSP's presence felt in Andhra Pradesh. He wants a similar situation to be repeated elsewhere in the coming Assembly elections. Hung Assemblies, with strong BSP presence is what he wants. This, I fear, is a purely negative policy and not a comprehensive and constructive policy of creating a society based on egality, freedom and justice. The status of Mulayam Singh's Samajvadi Dal is similar, and its attempt to strike roots in other States are not likely to achieve great results. Kanshi Ram continues to heep humiliation on Mulayam Singh almost daily. The OBC-SC/ST alliance does not work smoothly. There are within it latent conflicts of economic interest and status. Neither the BSP nor the SP have any plans for mitigating these conflicts. Aggravation of social and caste tension cannot be equated with the abolition of caste. Neither Kanshi Ram nor Mulayam Singh has pondered deeply over this problem.

Assam is a mosaic of ethnic, linguistic and religious groups. It was rocked by tribal revolts, and the Assamese-Bengali disturbances in the early sixties. In the course of time Negaland, Meghalaya, Mizoram and Arunachal were constituted into separate States. The anti-outsider agitation in Assam of the early eighties led to the formation of a Regional party called the Assam Gana Parishad. After the Assam Accord of 1985, it emerged successful in the polls. But its younger leaders demonstrated no conspicuous aptitude for administration and so the disillusioned electorate voted the Congress back to power. The conditions in Assam, however, continue to be disturbed, and the threat of Ulfa and Bodo terrorism is driving out businessmen from the State. The economy of Assam is fast going downhill. The small North-eastern States also have not been particularly successful in economic matters. Unemployment grows daily, and the widespread and mindless deforestation threatens to produce an ecological disaster. So far neither the Congress nor the Regional parties of the North-east have given evidence of their ability to cope with the difficult problems of the region in general and of the individual States in particular.

The only durable regional parties appear to be the Akali Dal, the Dravida parties in Tamil Nadu and, perhaps, N.T. Rama Rao's Telugu Desam. Even Assam Gana Parishad, as pointed out above, appears to be a passing phenomenon.

The Akali Dal is the oldest of these parties. Its birth can be traced to the Movement for the Liberation of the Gurudwaras from the clutches of the Mahants in the early twenties. The Akali Dal has had a chequred political career. Sometimes it had close relations with the Congress, sometimes a gulf opened between the two.

In the elections to the Punjab Provincial Assembly in 1937 the Akali Dal made an agreement with the Congress which covered 24 Sikh seats. The Akali Dal was to contest 14 out of these 24 seats and 10 were left to Sikh Congressmen. Just as in the early years many Muslims participated in the Sessions of both the Muslim League and the Indian National Congress, so also some Sikhs and Hindus also maintained their association both with INC and their communal Parties—the Akali Dal and Hindu Mahasabha. It is interesting to note that among the fourteen Akali candidates in 1937 were such men as Sardar Swaran Singh and Sardar Pratap Singh Kairon alongside of Sardar Baldev Singh and Giani Kartar Singh. Sardar Swaran Singh is known as a veteran Congressman who filled many posts in the State and, especially, the Central Government. Pratap Singh Kairon was for many years the Congress Chief Minister of Punjab and was known to have put down the Akalis with a heavy hand. Baldev Singh became the Defence Minister in the Interim Government and the Giani emerged as an importnt Akali politician. In the 1946 elections, however, there was no Congress-Akali agreement. The Congress won 10 Sikh constituencies, and all the other 23 seats were captured by the Akali Dal. The Congress, thus, could claim the support of not a negligible section of the Sikhs. In the Second General Election under the Nehru-Master Tara Singh Pact, the Akali Sikhs accepted the Regional Formula and merged in the Congress *politically*. In the 1962 elections the Congress and Akalis again opposed each other.

The removal of the Chief Minister Pratap Singh Kairon crippled the Congress. The formation of the Punjabi Suba and the general anti-Congress wave enabled the Akalis to improve their position. With the help of other non-Congress Parties the Akalis formed coalition Governments under Justice Gurnam Singh's and Prakash Singh Badal's leadership (1967, 1969, 1970 and 1977). But these did not last. The Congress had in the meanwhile embarked on a dangerous course. After 1977 it began to encourage the Sikh militants to destroy the Akalis. That Bhindranwale was a creation of Sanjay Gandhi and his men is no secret. The Akalis became badly divided. But now Sikh fundamentalism, which had received a fillip, spread terror far and wide. As a consequence of Congress factionalism, which afflicted the Darbara Singh's Government in 1980-82, and the rampant terrorism, the public life of Punjab was destroyed.

The Rajiv-Longowal Pact led nowhere. It had certain negative features. The bane of the Akali, Sikh and Punjab politics is its domination by religion—not in the form of ethical principles or moral order, but in the sense of bigotry and communalism. The SGPC Act, enacted under British rule, has been a destructive force. By centralising control of Gurudwaras in Punjab, it put enormous resources and power in the hands of religious leaders.These leaders have never used this power wisely. These last many years they have been demanding the passage of an all-India Act. Rajiv Gandhi foolishly promised it. That would be a disaster. In fact the control of Gurudwaras needs to be decentralised to break the grip of fanatics over the funds. This decentralisation should be extended to the religious shrines of other denominations also.

The elections which followed the Accord put the Akali Dal in power *with an absolute majority for the first time.* But the Akalis had no will to fight terrorism. Longowal himself had been killed by the terrorists. (Later also Balwant Singh, the Finance Minister). The Barnala Government which assumed office, after Akali Dal's victory in the 1985 elections, dithered. Factionalism led to the secession of Amarendra Singh and Badal. Finally, Rajiv Gandhi had no choice but to dismiss the Barnala Government. Terrorism had now degenerated into crime. The people longed for peace. It was the disintegration of the Akalis and their boycott of the elections which provided an opportunity to the new Chief Minister Beant Singh, with the help of G.S. Gill, to bring terrorism under control. After more than a decade of senseless violence, peace has returned to Punjab. The militants perhaps, realise the futility of violence. But the situation is still precarious. The Akalis may be divided into 10 factions. But the Sikh sentiment is still not with the Congress. The operation Blue Star and the anti-Sikh riots of 1984—in fomenting which some Congress leaders in Delhi played a part—have tarnished the Congress image. The Akali prospects also in the imme-diate future are therefore bleak. How durable the present peace will be is a question which future alone can answer. *When will the Sikhs realise that their fate is bound up with India and that the people of this country wish to accord them a pride of place in their scheme of things?*

Another old Regional party is Tamil Nadu's Dravida Munnetra Kazhagam. Its precursors in the political field was the Justice Party and in the social field Periyar Ramaswamy Naicker's Self-Respect Movement and Dravidra Kazhagam. Both these forces wielded considerable influence in Tamil Nadu. But so powerful was the appeal of the national movement that when Provincial Autonomy was introduced in 1937 the Congress was able to inflict a crushing defeat on the Justice Party. Many elements were absorbed by the Congress and the Congress supremacy remained unchallenged for nearly three decades (1937-67). But a new regional challenge was taking shape in the form of Dravidra Munnetra Kazhagam whose leaders had broken away from the Periyar. Its rise was very rapid. In the first Assembly (of the then composite Madras Presidency) the Communists were the leading opposition group not only in the Andhra area but also in the Tamil-speaking parts. After the separation of Andhra Pradesh, the DMK began to gather strength. North versus South, Brahmin versus Non-brahmin and Hindi versus Tamil and English were its chief agitational planks. The Celluloid stars gathered around Annadurai's banner. In the 1962 elections the DMK surprised everybody by capturing 50 Assembly seats. It elected 8 members to the Lok Sabha. The translation of Kamaraj from Chief Ministership of Tamil Nadu (then Madras) to the Presidentship of the Congress was a windfall for the DMK. The border war with China aroused patriotic fervour from which the DMK was not immune. The Constitution came to be amended to ban secessionism and the DMK gave up its separatist plank. Thereafter the DMK stressed only State Autonomy and not secession and began to make rapid strides. In the anti-Hindi agitation of 1965 it achieved a breakthrough.

It was the Satyamurthi-Kamaraj group which had marginalised Rajaji in the nineteen forties. He was finally pushed out in 1954. *The DMK, now blessed by Rajaji,* forged a mighty anti-Congress front, drawing in the Swatantra Party, the Muslim League and the Communists, and in 1967 the Congress suffered a heavy electoral defeat. Not only C. Subramaniam, a Central Minister, lost, but Kamaraj himself was defeated by a young DMK man. Probably the magnitude of the Congress debacle came as a surprise to Annadurai. He had stood as a parliamentary candidate. If he had been confident of winning a majority in the Assembly he would not have sought election to Parliament. In the event Annadurai was elected the Leader of the DMK Party in the Assembly, became Chief Minister, fought an Assembly bye-election and gave up his membership of the Lok Sabha.

The death of Annadurai placed the leadership in the hands of Karunanidhi. He responded to Indira Gandhi's initiative and made a pact with her in the 1971 mid-term Lok Sabha and Assembly polls. The Congress withdrew from the Assembly elections and supported the DMK. By 1972 the first rumblings of revolt within the DMK were heard and the Celluloid hero, M.G. Ramachandran, broke away from the DMK. The Congress-DMK relations became strained and Karunanidhi was dismissed in 1976. A new alliance of the Congress and MGR swept the polls in Tamil Nadu in 1977. But when the Congress failed to win power at the Centre MGR began to gravitate towards the Janata Party (1970-1980). Indira Gandhi was displeased. A reversal of alliances was executed in Tamil Nadu and in the 1980 polls the erstwhile enemies—the Congress and the DMK—again became friends. *The Tamil voters conscious of the importance of stability at the Centre voted for Mrs. Gandhi, although for the State Assembly elections it continued to prefer MGR's party.* The death of MGR and the split in the AIADMK led to the premature 1989 poll in which the Congress and the two AIADMK factions fought separately and lost out to the DMK. This election showed that the Congress could only be an auxiliary force in Tamil Nadu and not a major actor. The Janaki faction of the AIADMK soon faded out, leaving the field to Ms. Jayalalitha. The DMK Government was removed by Chandra Shekhar—presumably under her pressure—and the 1991 polls saw the revival of the Congress-AIADMK alliance. *The Tamil Nadu electorate has, it would seem quite deliberately, resolved to combine vote for Central stability with the articulation of the States' special interests through a Regional party.* The first objective Tamil Nadu has attained by voting for the Congress-Regional Party alliance in the parliamentary elections held in 1971 and 1980 (with the DMK), and 1985 and 1991 (with AIADMK). Only once did the voters miscalculate. While India's North-west, North, Centre, East and West voted against the Congress in 1977, the Tamil Nadu voters opted for the Congress-AIADMK alliance. The mistake was rectified by the electorate in the subsequent Lok Sabha elections.

Tamil Nadu was held to be, some decades ago, one of the best administered States in the country. But as elsewhere administration has deteriorated in this State also. Personality Cult and the usual nexus of politics-bureaucracy-police-crime have taken a heavy toll of administrative efficiency and law and order.

In weaving the complex multi-coloured fabric that is India; Tamil Nadu's contribution has been quite significant. Despite the atheist, anti-North, secessionist propaganda the people of Tamil Nadu continue to be profoundly religious. They are devoted to national unity in their own way. Tamil Nadu is a land of pilgrim centres of all-India importance like Kanchipuram, Srirangam, Rameswaram and so on. It boasts of more splendid temples than any other part of India. Sit quietly for a few hours in the magnificent temple of Brihadeswar at Tanjavoor and you will know what makes India tick. I myself saw some Muslims, including Muslim women, in the throng of devotees and visitors. Among South Indian pilgrims to Kashi and Badri-Kedar, Tamils easily outnumber others. You cannot conceive of the Indian Union without Tamil Nadu anymore than you can conceive of it without other States. Its consistent support to Regional parties does not mean that its people are not concerned about the nation's unity.

The most spectacular rise of a Regional party in recent years has undoubtedly been that of the Telugu Desam of Andhra Pradesh. It was formed by N.T. Ram Rao, a major celluloid figure who had achieved fame by playing the roles of mythological heroes. The first Convention of Telegu Desam was held on 11 April 1982. The second Convention took place soon after, that is on 22 May 1982. Thereafter NTR undertook an intensive tour of the State. He had a punishing schedule, addressing 30-40 meetings a day. His ability to attract crowds, especially poor people and women, surpassed that of Indira Gandhi. The meteoric rise of the silver screen hero cannot be explained only in terms of his personality. True he was a good communicator and played on the heartstrings of the Telugu people. Myths, old astrological forecasts, in brief everything that was serviceable was skilfully utilised by this master of PR. But inspite of his undoubted gifts the Cinestar would not have been able to win over the people of Andhra Pradesh had not a widespread and deep revulsion alienated the Telugu-speaking people from the Congress. From 1952 to 1955 it had appeared that the main threat to the Congress would emanate from the Communist Party. The separate Andhra State was established in 1953. Although the Congress had successfully enticed T. Prakasam away from the PSP, the Ministry was not stable. A new election became inevitable. In the 1955 election to the Andhra Assembly the united CPI mounted a strong offensive against the Congress. But it was beaten back and thereafter for nearly three decades the Congress dominated the Government and politics of Andhra Pradesh.

The decline of the Communist Movement in Andhra Pradesh—there were two successive splits within its ranks, first in the united CPI and then in the CPI-M—blunted the Communist challenge. There was a vacuum in the Andhra Pradesh Opposition politics. The Congress had done poorly in the Telugu-speaking areas of Madras and Hyderabad States in the First General Election to the Lok Sabha and State Assemblies. But in the Second General Election to the Lok Sabha held after the formation of the united State of Andhra Pradesh it polled 51.5 per cent vote. It never looked back. In the Fifth General Election to the Lok Sabha its share of the popular vote was 55.7 per cent. In the historic 1977 Lok Sabha election Andhra Pradesh stood by the Congress and gave it 57.4 per cent vote. The Janata Party-CPI-M alliance under Sanjiva Reddy could secure only one seat out of Andhra Pradesh's quota of 42 seats. In the Assembly polls also the Congress did well in all these years. There was another split in the Congress in 1978. But neither the Janata Party nor Vengal Rao's Congress could prevail against the great Amma. Indira Gandhi repeated her amazing success in the 1980 Lok Sabha poll.

What was it that happened in the term of the Assembly elected in 1978 that turned the Andhra people against Indira Gandhi? The biggest factor was the game of musical chairs the Congress-I played in that State. After the 1978 poll Chenna Reddy of the Indira Congress had taken over from Vengal Rao. He was replaced by T. Anjaiah on 11 October 1980. The prestige of the Office of Chief Minister plumeted. Anjaiah was publicly humiliated by Rajiv Gandhi, a mere General Secretary. He was displaced within less than 18 months by Venkatarama Reddy (24 February 1982). This Chief Minister did not last even for seven months. Vijay Bhaskara Reddy was brought in on 19 September 1982. The people were offended. Their pride was deeply hurt. *The contempt shown by the Centre towards the Andhra Chief Ministers was taken as an insult by the electorate.* The incessant demands of the Central Congress for money, and corruption of the Andhra Pradesh Congress politicians scandalised everybody. The backward classes, Harijans and women moved away from the Congress. It was this psychological moment which NTR seized. The people responded enthusiastically. In the trial of strength in January 1983 the Congress-I was trounced by NTR's Telugu Desam.

It was a great pity that the Congress leadership—Indira Gandhi, Rajiv Gandhi and their close advisers—refused to draw any lesson from their defeat in Andhra Pradesh and Karnataka. Neither did they consider changing their style of running the State Party organizations and the Congress Legislature Parties nor the manner of managing the Centre-State relations at the Governmental level. When power slipped from their hands in Andhra Pradesh they had recourse to their tactics of the 1967-69 period of encouraging defection by offering the defectors loaves and fishes of office. Nadendla Bhaskar Rao had been an early supporter of N.T. Rama Rao. Displeased by the Chief Minister's functioning, he opened secret negotiations with the Congress-I. The Governor was privy to these talks. When the dissidents gathered "sufficient strength", the Governor, at the instance of Rajiv Gandhi and Arun Nehru, dismissed Rama Rao and installed Bhaskar Rao as Chief Minister. According to what G.P. Moopnar told me, after his return from Hyderabad, the Indira Gandhi strategy was to let the revolt gather strength and *bring about the fall of Rama Rao on the floor of the Assembly*. But Bhaskar Rao and the Andhra Pradesh Governor were in a hurry and when they got clearance from Rajiv Gandhi and Arun Nehru, they acted. That created a storm not only in the State but throughout the country. Of late Rama Rao's popularity was visibly going down. But the abuse of the Governor's power at the behest of the Congress-I, created a sympathy wave for N.T. Rama Rao. The Opposition rallied around the Telugu Desam and the Congress-I had to retrace its steps and submit to public opinion. Then came the Lok Sabha elections. Rama Rao dissolved the unreliable Assembly and punished the defectors.

In 1977 almost the whole country was against the Indira-led Congress. But the Southern States, and especially Andhra Pradesh, stood by her. Now in 1985, the whole country, shaken by Mrs. Gandhi's assassination, voted for the Congress-I, but so angry were the Andhra Pradesh voters that the Congress-I was swept away in the Telugu Desam avalanche and out of the 42 Lok Sabha seats the Congress could secure only six seats. The TDP got 30 parliamentary seats and for the first time in the history of the Lok Sabha an avowedly Regional party became the largest Opposition Party in the House. The performance of the Rama Rao Ministry was lacklustre and after completing his five-year term the control of the State passed into the hands of the Congress again. The Congress ascendancy was confirmed by the 1991 Lok Sabha poll.

It appears that Rama Rao is quite hopeful of returning to power in 1995. But there are three complicating factors of assending importance : the internal discontent (Renuka), the BSP and the Kapus.

The case study of the three main regional parties underlines the paradox that while an integrated national party is a must for holding this country of vast diversity together, a unitary national party tends to ignore the legitimate aspirations of the States for autonomous functioning—in party as well as in governmental affairs. The central domination is widely resented and sometimes even assumes self-defeating violent forms. Where the people perceive that a great injustice has been done—as in Punjab in 1969 and Andhra Pradesh in 1984—people take electoral revenge at the next opportunity. *But sometimes the people also do think that the Central intervention is not unwarranted.* In 1991 the Tamil Nadu voters did not support the DMK whose Government had been dismissed. Similarly when a State Government belonging to a highly centralised party deliberately challenges the constitutional order, as the BJP did in UP on 6 December 1992, then recourse to President's rule under Article 356 becomes inevitable. *The results showed that the people did not dissent from the Centre's action.*

Another reason for the rise of Regional parties from time to time is the rampant warlordism of powerful and egoistic local leaders based on community, caste, and linguistic solidarity. The warlords are a law unto themselves. They thrive on fancied or real popular grievances. Unless the legitimate grievances are removed and the voters also become more discriminating, warlordism will not disappear.

I consider the rise of chauvinistic political groups based on linguism, communalism and regionalism (Shiv Sena, Ulfa, ISS and so on) as a symptom of the malfunctioning of the political system, not as a sign of its strength. Personally, therefore, I am not at all sanguine, as some academic political scientists and sociologists are, about a loose confederation of regional leaders, with their super egos, coming together to run the country and preserve its unity. *I believe the good of the country lies in enacting a German type law on political parties,* in democratising their functioning, compulsory revelation of the sources of their income and curb on the power of the so-called charismatic leaders in party choosing candidates for the various representative bodies.

In view of the complexities discussed above, it is not profitable, I think, to discuss the question of the State Autonomy as against the Centre's supremacy in abstract terms. We Indians do not possess the Anglo-Saxon genius for compromise, for working together. Unfortunately, we tend to go to the extreme. We have not pursued consciously and deliberately the middle path, till it has become a second nature. As long as this does not happen, the Central Government cannot be wholly disarmed constitutionally vis-a-vis the States. And unless and until the Centre learns to behave and to foster the States with loving care, Regional parties would not disappear nor would protests and revolts, whether violent or democratic and peaceful, against the excesses of the Centre cease. A very ambivalent and rather melancholy conclusion this, I confess.

27

THE BJP'S NEW PLOY

A subtle shift seems to be in the offing in the political line of the BJP. The RSS *Pariwar* has apparently outgrown the euphoric phase that began with L.K. Advani's *Rathyatra* in the second half of 1990 and climaxed with the mid-1991 Lok Sabha and Assembly polls. The BJP leaders were dazzled by their spectacular electoral success. They had increased their Lok Sabha representation from 89 in 1989 to 119 in May-June 1991. They had won 51 per cent vote in the Gujarat Lok Sabha elections. They had annexed the UP Assembly, and had secured 50 out of a total 85 Lok Sabha seats in that State. In Karnataka where the BJP was virtually non-existent, it had forged ahead of the well-entrenched Janata Dal of R.K. Hegde and S.R. Bommai, annexing a substantial chunk of 28 per cent vote. The Central power then seemed within easy grasp, either through a short-term coalition with the Congress or on the basis of an outright victory in the fresh Lok Sabha election which it expected could not be far off.

"Non-Congressism is dead", declared a self-intoxicated Advani. "Hereafter, it is the BJP *versus* the rest". If the BJP was euphoric, the Janata Dal and other secular parties were utterly demoralised. The JD leader in the Rajya Sabha also thought that non-Congressism was not relevant anymore. Even the prophet V.P. Singh was so unnerved that he also talked of an "anti-BJP front". In an interview to *The Sunday Mail*, V.P. Singh said that it was the J.D. which was setting the agenda for the Government. Really, it was our programme and the Congress Ministers were only signing. He was also generally supportive of Dr. Manmohan Singh's liberalisation programme. After all who had given the *final* clearance to the Pepsi Cola deal ? Was it not the V.P. Singh Government which did that ? V.P. Singh, therefore, told the *The Sunday Mail* that they should be ready for the challenge of the international market and competition, only that they should be caring towards labour.[1]

Bhaurao Devras's (RSS Joint General Secretary's) idea of a coalition did not take off the ground.[2] But there was cooperation of sorts between the Ruling Congress and the BJP. The BJP was offered the Deputy Speakership. There were talks on Ayodhya. The Advanis, Jaswant Singhs and Promod Mahajans were even more enthusiastic about liberalisation than V.P. Singh. L.K. Advani even undertook a tour of the Western World as non-official Economic Ambassador of the new P.V. Narsimha Rao Government. It is hypocrital on the part of BJP to pretend that they are against the GATT treaty. *Even a man of the meanest intelligence knows that globalisation and liberalisation are two sides of the same coin.*

The public memory is short, and the public has probably forgotten all these post-election utterances of Opposition leaders in 1991. The J.D. executive, of course, turned down the V.P. Singh suggestion of an anti-BJP front, and the Congress-BJP honeymoon, too, was over within eighteen months.

By July 1992 the Sangh Pariwar had returned to an aggressive posture on the Ayodhya issue. The higher courts came into the picture, and with very great difficulty the BJP could be persuaded to desist from adopting a programme of open defiance. The Sangh Pariwar, finally, announced its Kar Seva Action Plan on 6th December. The Supreme Court extracted an assurance from the BJP's UP Government. The affidavit was filed. But the sequence of events proved that for the Sangh Pariwar it was only a subterfuge. A wrecking squad was trained secretly. The Central Home Minister's request for the deployment of Central Police Forces was turned down. On 6th December 1992 all the roads leading to the Kar Seva site were blocked at L.K. Advani's instance. *At least by 5 December 1992 L.K. Advani, RSS General Secretary H.R. Shashadri and Ashok Singhal had become privy to the real nature of the Action Plan.*

The event of 6th December shocked everybody. The entire non-

BJP opposition condemned the act of vandalism. Even the Congress was rudely awakened from its slumber. President's Rule was imposed not only in UP but in the other three BJP-ruled states also. The Proclamation was strongly supported by the non-BJP opposition.

Now in the name of forming a united front against the GATT Final Act it appears that Chandra Shekhar and George Fernandes are laying the basis for cooperation with the Sangh Pariwar which has a two-faced policy on this issue.

There was cooperation between BJP and JD till the middle of 1990. Nobody objected to that. The Left itself knew that the BJP's support was necessary for the Government's survival. It was when the BJP took up the Babri Masjid-Ram Janambhoomi issue in a big way that other parties were forced to demarcate themselves from the BJP. The BJP itself, as said above, proclaimed the death of non-Congressism. However, after the drubbing the Sangh Pariwar has received in the UP, MP and HP elections, the Sangh has begun to feel the impact of its isolation. Its dream of riding to central power has been shattered at least for the present. It is in desperate need of allies. It has offered joint action on GATT. The left has rejected the BJP overture. So has the Janata Dal. Even V.P. Singh, after his return from "exile", has said "no" to the BJP.

The BJP leaders have, after three years, again seen "some non-Congress space" in Indian politics. Govindacharya is harking back to the spirit of 1974. As *The Hindu* reported : "On coordination with other parties, the BJP general secretary, K. Govindacharya said : 'The ball is in the other court.' We would like to work together (with the other political parties on the anti-Dunkel issue), *we hope a JP-type of movement will be built up*. The BJP agitation could also lead to a call for civil disobedience but the political situation would determine the timing of this, he said. Govindacharya was strongly critical of the Left parties, saying "classical marxist tools cannot be used in the Indian context."[3]

Another report said : "New Delhi, April 13 : *The BJP strategists have rediscovered the virtues of anti-Congressism in the face of the realisation that the Hindutva plank in itself may not be sufficient to pole vault the party into the power.......* Having assesed that the Hindutva lacunae will not be ironed out in a hurry, the BJP leaders have decided that the proclamation that the party had become one of the poles in politics was premature. Realising that actual grouping together of anti-BJP forces would create a serious problem, the Hindutva strategists believe there exists sufficient 'anti-Congress' space in the country.[4] This is an instance of their complete cynicism. Only the naive or the knaves will trust them. Their latest championship of Swadeshi is a ploy. Their middle class following is consumerist to the core and is fond of foreign brand names and goods. The appetites of this middle class are insatiable. It is significant that long before the name Aurther Dunkel was heard of and GATT Treaty signed, the foreign brand names and foreign companies held sway here in the low technology area of toothpastes, shaving creams and lotions. What prevented Indian industry from pushing them out through low costs, low prices and high quality? How can the Sangh Pariwar's new plank of cooperation be considered sincere? If they are honest, they would have abandoned their plan of siezing religious shrines. But they are not prepared to do that. The new RSS Chief is repeatedly asserting the Pariwar's determination to take possession of Ayodhya, Kashi and Mathura sites. The tone is increasingly becoming strident. Some BJP leaders' rhetoric has recently scaled new heights of absurdity and hatred. Uma Bharti will allow reconstruction of the Babri Mosque only if a temple of Hanuman is allowed to be built at Mecca! The West Bengal BJP President threatens to invade and annex Bangladesh if it opposes deportation of illegal immigrants.[5] *If Bangladesh really becomes part of India, legal immigration-will turn into a flood.* Anybody who takes up their offer of joint action, without insisting on the Sangh Pariwar's completely turning its back on the past four years' disgraceful history, would be helping *not* the cause of preserving the economic sovereignty of India but in digging the grave of the constitutional democratic order. Only those whose lodestar is power politics will, I think, walk into the spider's parlour.

References

1. *The Sunday Mail*, 24-30 November 1991.
2. *The Times of India*, 27 November 1991.
3. *The Hindu*, 12 April 1994.
4. *The Telegraph*, 14 April 1994.
5. *The Telegraph*, 22 April 1994.

Section V

INDO-RUSSIAN RELATIONS

28

AMERICAN FEAR OF A GERMAN-RUSSIAN ENTENTE

The Russian Federation, the largest constituent of the Soviet Union, is in deep turmoil. The reports on the conditions in Yeltsin's Russia in the Western press are invariably adverse. They relate to the unprecedented inflation, growth in crime, prostitution and rise of the separatist movements in the Russian Federation. The old bureaucrats remain in power everywhere. But they no longer talk Red. They have turned White. There is no positive reporting on the economy. No observer speaks of a smooth transition from a centralised command economy to a market economy, of the increase in production and productivity, the appearance of new dynamic entrepreneurs, and of the successful privatisation of the old stagnant collectivised agriculture. Their conclusion is that none of these things has materialised in Russia.

The real cause of the present tragic condition of Eastern Europe, including Russia, is that while their resentment against one-party rule and the failure of the Centralised Planned Economy to deliver the goods the consumers desired was legitimate, in their fury they also destroyed the positive features of the Soviet order such as the system of social security which it provided for the war veterans, the pensioners, the old and the infirm and, above all, the protection to children in the matter of education and health. Now the Social Security system lies in ruins.

There were many dire predictions about famine deaths in the former USSR, two years ago. They spoke of Russia's terminal illness. And yet Russia has survived all these calamities. The Russians are an extremely vital people. Their capacity for self-suffering is limitless. Their ability to survive calamities of a colossal magnitude has been proved again and again. What other people would have overcome the agony of defeat in the First World War and the ordeal of a prolonged civil war? What other people would have put up with the massacre of the peasantry, and the continuing terrible purges under Stalin's long rule? What other nation would have survived the four-year holocaust of Nazi invasion and slaughter in which more than 20 million people perished? Only a sturdy people could have done that. I believe in the Russian people's dynamism and I am confident that the present crisis would not last beyond a decade or two and then Russia would step forth as a powerful nation again.

Although the end of the cold war and the collapse of the Soviet system created a unipolar world, the American Foreign Policy Establishment has not achieved "Freedom from Fear". A Japanese-American celebrated the triumph of liberal democracy even by pronouncing *The End of History*[1]. Yet the establishment is haunted by several ghosts,some imaginery, some real. One writer predicted the beginning of a civilizational conflict in place of the War of Nations or their Coalitions. Some others were haunted by the fear of Japan's growing economic power. Yet others are afraid of China's becoming a mighty power in the next few decades. But there is a class of American diplomats and Foreign Policy scholars who refuse to shed their fear of the Russian successor of the USSR's military power and inheriter of its vast natural resources. The unification of the two Germanies, which was the direct result of the disintegration of the Soviet system, have aroused in the American ideologists of geopolitics, the fear of a resurgent Germany's alliance with a Russia which has recouped its economic and diplomatic strength. In fact this dread goes back to the days of the Hitler-Stalin Pact of August 1939 or even the earlier Rapallo Treaty between "the two outcaste nations" (Germany and Bolshevik Russia) signed in 1922. It had been lying dormant since the out-break of the titanic Nazi-Soviet conflict in June 1941. Dormant indeed this fear was for fifty years, but it never disappeared, and has begun to surface once again.

There was a powerful school of "geopolitics" in Germany in the interregnum between the First and Second World Wars of which

K. Haushofer was a leading exponent. There is a lot of prejudice against the expression and the thinking it represents among certain intellectual circles, including Marxist thinkers, although there is nothing sinister about the term and the USSR itself had been a practitioner of geopolitics in its heyday. Geopolitics, properly understood, it is equivalent to a realistic world view. It takes into account the influence of geography, climate, soil conditions, natural resources, strategic situation and so on on international politics. Henry Kissinger was quite fond of using this expression, sometimes to confound his critics and sometimes to hide his real movtives. Here I wish to have a look at the views of the German Karl Haushofer on German foreign policy. Haushofer and people of his way of thinking looked upon the USSR, in the early twenties, as being another pariah nation which had also been geographically mutilated and then rejected by the West. Together, said Haushofer, the two powers (Germany and Russia) could form the "continental union of the expelled against the sea-ruling world-power in the League of Nations." There was another strand of this policy. Japan had always been one of Haushofer's principal loves and fascinations. He now watched the rise of Japanese imperial power with much admiration and he saw in Japan a state from which Germany could learn a great deal. At an early stage he became convinced that Japan had to be a friend and not an enemy in his country's challenge to the fateful Anglo-American hegemony. Earlier he had written that together Japan, Russia and the Central European Power (Germany) would be absolutely unassailable as they were "the only group of powers able to defend itself against the Anglo-Saxon tutelege". Thus Haushofer was very much a man of Rapallo and in 1939 he was to be equally enthusiastic over the Nazi-Soviet pact.[2]

After reunification the German outlook is undergoing a change. The united Germany is a non-nuclear power, and is still a member of Nato. But its passivity in foreign affairs is already a thing of the past. *It showed its new clout by forcing Western recognition of the Roman Catholic Slovenia and Croatia who had declared their independence from Yugoslavia.* Increasingly it is turning towards Eastern Europe and Russia for expansion of commercial, industrial, scientific and cultural contacts. That is why the ghost of Haushofer is haunting some Americans and they are stridently demanding the strengthening of the Nato system. This is necessary to "constrain a revisionist or plainly expansionist new Russia, and, discreetly, also to limit the freedom of manoeuvre of a more self-assertive Germany", Bilinsky has written. A united Germany can no longer be taken for granted as a docile member of the Western alliance. Being a strong power in the heart of Europe, it was bound to radiate its political and economic influence both Eastward and Westward, men like Bilinsky think.[3] Their advice to the American Presidents and Congress is to evolve a long term perspective to cope with the aforesaid incipient development which they are afraid would flower out fully in a decade or so.

The fears of the Bilinksys does not mean that a German-Russian-Japanese alliance has become a reality. No, it has not. Nor does it mean that there are no conflicts of interests between these three countries or that there are no contradictions bedevilling the Russo-Japanese or Russo-Chinese or Sino-Japanese relations. *But fear itself is a potent force and might lead America into policies that would make some of the imaginary fears come true.*

It is against these new developments—the gradual shift of economic power to Eastern (and South-eastern Asia) and the growing predominance of the united Germany—that I have been urging the revamping of our foreign policy establishment and its reeducation, emphasising the transformation of our private and public sector companies into transnational companies, to have a section of the personnel in our Embassies in these newly emerging countries fully equipped with trade and technological expertise. *While seeking constant improvement of the Indo-American relations, we should not neglect the united Germany, E.U. and Japan.* We must persuade the Chinese to demarcate the line of control on the ground and strengthen mutually beneficial relationship. Non-governmental groups can approach China and urge upon it to make up with Tibet and Dalai Lama and thereby pre-empt meddling by the United States.

References

1. Francis Fukuyama, *The End of History, The National Interest.* Summer 1989, pp. 3-18
2. Geoffery Parker, *Western Geopolitical Thought in the Twentieth Century*, 1985, London, pp. 58-66
3. *Russia and America From Rivalry to Reconciliation.* Editors: George Ginsburg, Alvin Z. Rubinstein, and Oles M. Smolansky, 1993, New York, Article by Yaroslav Bilinsky, at p. 229.

29

NARASIMHA RAO'S RUSSIAN VISIT : AN ASSESSMENT

P.V. Narasimha Rao has expressed his satisfaction with his first visit to Russia as Prime Minister. But no objective assessment of the long term effect of the trip can be made on the basis of one side's subjective satisfaction about its outcome nor on the basis of some of the expressions used in the Russo-Indian Communique. Thus the Joint Statement had "firmly" declared that it was "inadmissible to arouse inter-ethnic and inter-religious hatred or to promote aggressive nationalism or religious fanaticism." While other phrases hold good for both India and Russia, the words "aggressive nationalism" has application to the specific Russian situation. Russia feels that the outbreak of "aggressive nationalism" in Ukraine or Moldava or Latvia will not only spell disaster for the Russian minority but, as Peter Struve had predicted, it would lead to a schism in the Russian nation and be a disaster for the state. Even in the palmy days of Indo-Soviet relations the two countries' interests were not identical. These interests were non-conflicting in most areas of world policy, and, on some important issues, there was a striking convergence. But the Soviet Union's position was vastly different from that of Russia today.

The future of Russo-Indian relations would depend upon whether the Russians perceive that there is the same convergence of interests of the two countries as in the past. To my mind the Russians are deeply immersed in their own problems. In external relations their priority is the cultivation of good relations with the United States and other Western countries, (especially Kozyrev's), and the former constituents of the Soviet Union. In fact ties with the latter are of even greater importance from the Russian viewpoint *today*. The Russian euphoria about America has by now considerably evaporated, although it has to pay attention to its Western policy. Russia is naturally much concerned about its relations with the former sister Republics. Not only it had close organic ties with these Republics the latter contain a considerable Russian minority. This "minority" is very large in Kazakstan and Latvia; and not negligible in several other Republics. There is a sharp ethnic and religious divide between the populations of the Central Asian Republics and Russia. But that is not the case with Ukraine and Belarus. All three are Slav and predominantly Orthodox Christians in belief, although Ukraine has its Uniate Church, with links with the West, and its own Orthodox Church resents domination by the Russian Orthodox Church.

The Soviet state was not a *Russian* state. Apart from the use of the Russian tongue for the centralised government, the Soviet supra-national state was unable to create deep loyalty among its citizens. How fragile the Soviet bond was, has been demonstrated by the rapid and total collapse of the Soviet Union. The disruption after the disastrous *coup de'tat* of August 1991 was so devastating that even Ukraine, which had *freely* voted by more than 70 per cent for a union only a few months ago, was convulsed by the wave of nationalism and opted for total independence. This created the unresolved issues of Crimea, the division of the Black Sea Fleet and transfer of nuclear weapons stationed on Ukranian soil. The border between the Russian Federation and Ukraine did not coincide with the linguistic and ethnic divide, and this is true of most sister Republics. The Crimea region is preponderantly Russian and had been arbitrarily transferred to Ukraine by Nikita Khruschev in the fifties. Hence the phrases used in the Joint Declaration quoted above.

Like Russia, the Chinese People's Republic, too, is confronted with ethnic-religious diversity. A constituent Province of the Chinese Republic, Xinjiang (Chinese Turkestan) is predominantly Muslim. In China proper, too, there are the North-western Provinces which have a substantial Muslim presence. In November 1992 Russian and Chinese Foreign Ministers met. Kozyrev said that Central Asia should not be allowed to be dominated by "extremist and Islamic fundamentalist forces." Qian Qichen responded by talking of their common interests in upholding "stability" in Central Asia. The Moscow Declaration echoes the same sentiment.

But the common interest in maintaining the integrity of the multi-religious states based on toleration and secularism *does not necessarily imply convergence of strategic and economic interests.* From the days of Gorbachev himself, Moscow had been supporting the nuclear non-proliferation policy. The new Russia is not likely to give up that policy. It is doubtful, therefore, whether Prime Minister Rao was able to sell to President Yeltsin India's alternative line of *worldwide nuclear disarmament as against mere regional non-proliferation* which the United States favours. Russia's not joining the US in pressurising India would itself be a big gain.

Russia badly needs hard currency for its needs. Apart from oil, of which the production has been falling, what has Russia got to export except arms and defence equipment? Russia needs dollars. And driven by its hard currency needs, forgetting the past differences and future dangers, Moscow has been selling China defence equipment on a large scale. Russia has sold to China Sukhoi-27s, Sukhoi-31s, T-72 tanks, S-300 missiles and, what is more, technology to improve the accuracy of its delivery systems. Russia's desperate economic position compels it to seek an arms market in China. China's foreign exchange reserves enable it to give Russia dollars in exchange for defence equipment. Its talks with Pakistan on arms sales were motivated not by any anti-India bias, but the need for dollars. And the Atlanticists like Foreign Minister Kozyrev do not wish to treat India differently from Pakistan. Pakistan has access to the oil wealth of Saudi Arabia and other oil rich states. Whether the insight of strategic convergence and the compulsion of preserving the pluralistic order have led the Russian rulers to abandon the plan of sales of arms and defence material to Pakistan is more than can be stated with assurance. Even the Indian Prime Minister was somewhat evasive in his replies to questions put to him on the aircraft carrying the Rao party back home. The reason is not far to seek. With no signs of economic recovery, a tussle is going on in the Russian establishment between those who attach more importance to the pecuniary factor and others who are afraid of the danger of destabilisation caused by inter-ethnic and religious conflicts. Russian forces left Afghanistan, but Moscow has not been able to disengage from Tajikstan.

India cannot afford to rely wholly on the common ground of pluralism and ethnic peace. India must explore the possibility of expanding economic and trade relations with Russia. Wherever possible we should go in for joint ventures. Unless common economic ties again bind the two countries together, mere abstract principles and pious sentiments will not provide a strong foundation for friendship and cooperation. But it is a good sign that after the confusion of Indian policy in the wake of the *coup* of August 1991, our foreign policy establishment has begun to shed its old assumptions and prejudices and to take a fresh look at the new realities and accept the need for reconstructing the old Indo-Russian cooperation on a new basis.

The most worrisome aspect of the Indo-Russian economic relations is the problem of rubles and rupees. India's debt to the USSR amounts to Rs. 35000 crore. India is required to pay under the agreement Rs. 3000 crores yearly. This has to go on for 14 years. The repayment has to be in terms of traditional exports. But the Russia's old statist system of export-import and distribution has collapsed. The Russians are talking about allocation of the resources to their importers. The auction of rupees has been devised to met the difficulty of lack of resources. India's Commerce Minister sounds optimistic about the future. With wide fluctuations in Russian demand for tobacco, tea and leather products it is, however, difficult to gear the production here to Russian needs. There are similar problems with Ukraine which was the second most populous Republic within the former USSR. India should not neglect its ties with Ukraine or Kazakstan and other Central Asian Republics. A lot of ingenuity and application of mind is, I think, needed to sort out our tangled economic and trade relations with the constituents of the former centralised Soviet state.

INDEX

Adivasi, 136
Advani, L.K., 63, 165
Akali dal, 155
Ambedkar, Dr. B.R., 4, 14, 16
American foreign policy, 172
Amichand Pyarelal group of firms, 87
Annihilation of caste, 29
Assam, 7
Ayodhya, 108

Babri Masjid, 107
Bahujan Maha Sangh, 21
Bahaujan SAmaj Party, 21
Bhave, Vinoba, 127
Brailsford, H.N., 9
Brezhnev era, 1964-83, 57
British Conservative Party, 94
Bofors JPC Report, 87

Central Assembly, 6
Charkha, 66
Chavan, Y.B., 152
Chief Election Commission, 99
Chief Justice, Chagla, M.C., 84
Chinese People's Republic, 176
Coca-cola, 45
Code of Conduct, 124
Colonel Lanefax, 4
Commission of Inquiry, 82
Congress Party, 25
Constitutional Bench of the Supreme Court, 129

Dalits, 22
Dasyabhava, 27
Desai, Morarji, 139
Devi Lal, 116, 147
Devraj, 141
Dickens, Charles, 38
Dravidra Munnetra Kazhagam, 158
Dyarchy-Montgu-Chelmsford Reforms, 94

Federal Structure Committee, 8
Fernandes, George, 62, 167
Free Market Economy, 42

Gandhi, Indira, 95, 162
Gandhi, Mahatma, 11, 18
Gandhi, Rajiv, 25
Gandhi, Sanjay, 26
Gatt Final Act, 72
German Democratic Republic, 53
Gill, G.S., 157
God Apollo, 42
Good Terms, 39
Gothic Cathedral, 35
Greek orthodox, 35

Harijan, 8, 12
Harvard Business Review, 75
Hegde, R.K., 152
Hindu Society, 13
House of Commons, 1696, 36
Horabin, J.F., 9

Indian Penal Code, 113
Iron curtain, 44

Keshva, 150
Kamma party, 116
Khrushchev era, 57
Kissinger, Henry, 173
Krishnamachari, T.T., 82, 84
Kurmi's, 74

Labour party, 94
Laski, Harold, 9
Legislative Council in Maharashtra, 112
Life Insurance Corporation, 88
Lohia, Dr. Ram Manohar, 52
Lok Sabha, 110

Manu, Manuvad : Marxist party, 59